This book is presented to

Winnifred Herington

by

Donald G. Lawson

on behalf of the Board of Directors
of The Counselling Foundation of Canada

number __71__ of 250

A Coming of Age:

Counselling Canadians for Work in the Twentieth Century

with a foreword by Stephen Lewis

ISBN: 0-9687840-2-X

Published by
The Counselling Foundation of Canada
Toronto, Ontario, Canada
www.counselling.net

Distributed by
The Ginger Press
848 Second Avenue East
Owen Sound, Ontario Canada
N4K 2H3
www.gingerpress.com

Printed in Canada.

TABLE OF CONTENTS

Foreword by Stephen Lewis

I want to say that I don't pretend to know anything profound or substantial about the basic subject matter of career counselling. Therefore, I'm going to approach the theme in a rather more eclectic and generic way—weaving together a number of global and domestic strands and attempting to fashion some kind of symmetrical whole by the time I've reached the end.

Let me begin in this fashion. Later this week [January 2001], two remarkable international gatherings are taking place, which are directly linked even though they are continents apart. The first is called the World Economic Forum in Davos, Switzerland. All of the representatives of the major multinational corporations, the head of the International Monetary Fund, the head of the World Bank, the Secretary-General of the United Nations and the head of the World Trade organization will be there to etch an economic agenda for the next several years.

On precisely the same day, for the same purpose, there is gathering in Porto Allegre, Brazil at the World Social Forum, all of the social activists who were part of the anti-globalization protest movements. They represent vigorous critiques of democratic capitalist society and the processes they see unfolding.

What we really have then are two competing views of the way in which the world works. The one vision that is rooted in Davos, Switzerland is highly uncritical and romanticized. It is a vision which says that free market liberalization, private sector hegemony, dismantling of the public sector, trade liberalization, imposition of good governance on countries (particularly in the developing world), the fashioning of a financial architecture by the International Monetary Fund and the World Bank—that taken all together, these irresistible trends will mean a kind of panacea for humankind.

In Porte Allegro there is a quite different, somewhat inchoate view. These are people who look at the state of world poverty, who look at the state of environmental degradation, who see the social sectors atrophying, who watch human rights being abridged, who see that labour rights are nowhere prominently in place and feel that there has to be an alternative mandate for humankind.

Now, at the heart of this extraordinary debate are a number of bitter and brutal ironies. If globalization is so positive, then why are there so many identifiable and palpable global obscenities? Why are we dealing with a series of global problems for which there seems to be no global response?

Let me remind you, first, that the reality of contemporary and international poverty is deepening both within and among nations. The absolute numbers of people living in poverty in this world are growing annually. There are now 1.3 billion people living on less than $1.00 a day. There are 3 billion people living on less than $750.00 a year. And the world seems absolutely unable to intervene in a way which will do anything about it.

Number two, the HIV AIDS pandemic obviously cries out for global solution. I don't want to drive statistics through the wall but may I remind you that last year alone, there were 5.3 million new infections, 3.8 million of them in sub-Saharan Africa. Last year the number of people living with AIDS had risen to over 36 million world wide, 25 million of them living in sub-Saharan Africa. The number of deaths since the early 1980s when the pandemic began has now risen to over 21 million, 80 percent of them in sub-Saharan Africa.

Thirdly. Conflict is seizing the world in so many areas, from East Timor to Kosovo to the African continent. And let me remind you, it was seven years ago in Rwanda that 800,000 people were slaughtered in full view of the world. What kind of globalization is it that can't handle global imperatives like war and genocide? How can you talk about globalization in reasonable ways if the world can't gather itself to deal with identifiable obscenities of that kind?

I want to make mention of the environment. I picked up the *Globe and Mail* today and the headline states, "Scientists raise alarm of climate catastrophe." In Toronto in June of 1988, I chaired the first international conference on climate change where academics and social scientists and politicians from all around the world gathered to look at what was then an early and emerging phenomenon. The recommendations that flowed from that conference are exactly the recommendations which the world still embraces. And yet, no one adheres to them even though the International Panel on Climate Change recently released a report suggesting we are dooming humankind to perils we've not yet approximated.

And finally, in terms of these globalized problems for which we never seem to have global solutions, I want to mention in passing, the reality of the digital divide. There is an assumption that the technological and communications revolution of computers and the Internet are somehow going to alter the nature of international social justice, overcome disparity and make life livable for all of the developing world. Well, that assumption tends to forget that in countries like Ethiopia there are two telephone lines per thousand people and that more than half of the world's entire population has never made a phone call. So, until there are wireless and satellite systems in place absolutely everywhere, the assumptions we make about bringing developing countries on stream is so much intellectual claptrap.

All of these various themes which agitate internationalists constantly, came together at the Millennium Summit of the United Nations General Assembly in the fall of the year 2000 when, for the first time, the Secretary General of the United Nations, Kofi Anan, started speaking openly about globalization. He said:

"Few people, groups or governments oppose globalization as such. They protest against its disparities. First the benefits and opportunities of globalization remain highly concentrated among a relatively small number of countries and are spread unevenly within them. Second, in recent decades, an imbalance has emerged between successful efforts to craft strong and well-enforced rules facilitating the expansion of global markets while support for equally valid objectives, be they labour standards, the environment, human rights or poverty reduction has lagged behind. More broadly, for many people, globalization has come to mean greater vulnerability to unfamiliar and unpredictable forces that can bring on economic instability and social dislocation, sometimes at lightning speed. There is mounting anxiety that the integrity of cultures and the sovereignty of states may be at stake. Even in the most powerful countries, people wonder who is in charge, worry for their jobs and fear that their voices are drowned out in globalization's sweep."

It's quite fascinating how a number of leaders who mounted the platform of the General Assembly began to focus on the world of work and, of course, there is an organization in the international system which deals with the world of work, the International Labour Organization. The new head of the ILO, Juan Samovia, is for the first time from the developing world and someone who understands something about the class struggle. At a speech Juan made to the staff of the World Bank last year, he said:

"We know enough about market fundamentals. It's time to pay attention to the fundamentals in people's lives.

"At the beginning of the 1990s, I travelled widely preparing the agenda of the World Summit for Social Development. In multiple dialogues with civil society organizations, trade unions, business and governments, I inquired as to their country's principal social problems. In different formulations and styles, and equally valid in developed and developing countries, the answer was crisp and targeted. The problems were poverty and social exclusion. That is, poverty on the one hand and the exclusion from the main stream of so many of the minority and vulnerable groups in various societies.

"When I asked what was the solution, the answer was simple. Jobs.

"Yet the hard reality is that the benefits of globalization as it is currently unfolding are not reaching enough people. We know that the global economy is not creating enough jobs, and especially not enough jobs that meet peoples' aspirations for a decent life. The failure to improve both the quantity and quality of employment world wide is making working families afraid of a race to the bottom."

This is so very interesting. All of you are in a professional discipline where you focus inevitably on individual clients and on an effort to match individual capacities with the job market to fulfill people's work lives appropriately. And what I want to show you is that you're part, as it were, of an international movement.

Juan Samovia has been in his job barely a year. When he looked at the emphasis on employment, on career counselling, on the requirements, skills and otherwise for the world of work, he actually fashioned an alternative vision statement for the International Labour Organization. He called it simply "Decent Work." At a recent conference in Bangkok, this is how he defined it:

"Decent Work is not an intellectual idea. It is not merely a concept or notion. It is the most deeply felt aspiration of people in all societies, developed and developing. It's the way ordinary women and men express their needs.

"If you go out on the streets or in the fields and ask people what they want in the midst of the new uncertainties globalization has brought upon all of us, the answer is 'work.' Work on which to meet the needs of their families and safety and health, educate their children and offer them income security after retirement. Work in which they are treated decently and their basic rights are respected. That is what decent work is about and it's about reaching everyone. If you think about it, everybody works. Some of that work is done in large firms. Some of it is informal and a lot because it is done in the home, usually by women, and it is not even recognized as work. But all of those people have the right to decent work.

"To move in that direction, we must acknowledge that we share some basic values. So there is a universal social floor, one which we believe should apply everywhere because it is a question of basic human rights. Freedom from oppression and discrimination. Freedom of association. The right of children to learn and develop rather than to work. But decent work is more than that. Because it captures the aspirations, and possibilities of each society, reflecting different cultures, visions and development choices."

In Canada, we worry about putting people in the right jobs but you seldom hear cries of alarm about employment at large. We're kind of sanguine about these issues. And as a result, we're failing to understand some very tough imperatives about the eventual world of work.

Number one, Canada is way behind almost every other developed nation in its indifference to early childhood care and development even though we know that's when the best cognitive skills are being developed and when a child's emotional capacities are being reinforced. We have people like Fraser Mustard who provide whole agendas for early childhood care and development. But we don't have governments who pay any attention to it.

Second, we're doing almost nothing in this country about childcare, the centrepiece of an appropriate employment policy. Unless you're lucky enough to live in Quebec, your access to affordable childcare simply doesn't exist. Every single promise which has been made politically has resulted in a delinquent political implementation. And yet, how can you talk about a policy of decent work if you don't have childcare throughout the country?

Number three, education cutbacks are doing terrible damage to the kinds of people we want to emerge for the world of work, the kinds of people we want to be able to counsel. We're cutting back on music, on art, on heritage languages, on English as a Second Language and on Special Education. We are even abandoning libraries. We celebrate the triumphalism of computer technology at the expense of a broad liberal arts education. In your context, this gradually erodes any emphasis on multiculturalism, on diversity, on aboriginal rights, on the reality of dealing with people with disabilities and the way in which the work force can embrace such people. All of these things get undermined when your educational system is profoundly skewed by the cutbacks in education.

This leads me to my next point — that the cutbacks, generally through society and the social sectors are reaping havoc. We have such a twisted ideological rigidity of those who now run the political establishment. There's a kind of obsessive, compulsive support for debt reduction and then deficit reduction and then tax reduction but what of the human dimension? What about the social sectors? Why are we so absolutely obsessed with embracing this constant refrain that we are never able to find the money to invest in the social and human priorities?

We live in a profoundly altered environment. The economic culture is capricious. Jobs come and jobs go. It's really important to have lifelong learning. It's really important, I know, to understand the frailty of the manufacturing sector and the often disabling short-term jobs in the service industry. It's necessary to recognize that we've lost a lot of jobs to NAFTA and will continue to do so.

So, before your career counselling is authentic, it seems to me that we have to secure our approach. We have to focus on the economy as a whole—social sectors—as well as the economic and financial and corporate architecture. We have to understand that training and retraining is a legitimate pursuit of society. We have to recognize the value of early education and what it means down the years. We have to assess the global impacts that are occurring in terms of the job market in Canada.

We have to recognize, in the process, two fundamentals. One: Jobs that are rooted in and often originate from the community level are the jobs that are increasingly making sense internationally. I am fascinated by the way in which local community imperatives are taking prominence as a response to general economic trends everywhere. All over the world there is recognition that community-based work is work that is tremendously valuable and extremely well-rooted.

And the second thing, is advocacy. It isn't enough simply to counsel people into jobs. It's equally important to have entire disciplines, entire professions, entire career lines understand that there is an obligation to speak out against injustice. To take a stand on behalf of those you represent. Indeed, all of you who are attending this conference collectively, have a pretty strong position in this world and when you state your opinions, go to the barricades. Take up a cause. It has an impact on society.

And isn't that essentially what you are attempting to achieve—to make this world a more humane, just, civilized, decent environment? There is no objective, in human terms, in individual terms, more worthy of your notable commitment. I salute you.

Stephen Lewis
From the keynote address at
National Consultation on Career Development
Ottawa, Canada
22 January 2001

ACKNOWLEDGEMENTS

Many people from across Canada have given generously of their time and contributed valuable insights and information to *A Coming of Age*. In particular, we would like to thank our Advisory Group–Barry Adamson, Jean Faulds, Janis Foord Kirk, Sally Palmateer, Jo-Ann Sobkow, Marilyn Van Norman and Donna Walters–and our researchers–Nancy Anderson, Irene Canivet, Daniel J. Denis, Aaron De Maeser, Jo-Ann Sobkow and Pauline P. Wong for their help.

Our sincere appreciation and thanks also go to: Murray Axmith, Jan Basso, Sahri Woods Baum, Lyn Bezanson, Paul Boisvenue, Marilyn Burke, Dick Cappon, Colin Campbell, Marg Charlton, Jim Chisholm, Dave Clemens, F.J. Clute, Wendy Coffin, Stuart Conger, C. Cote, Keltie Creed, Laura Dokis-Kerr, Nancy Dube, Kay Eastham, Sy Eber, Laurie Edwards, Betty Egri, Robert Evans, Aryeh Gitterman, Jim Green, Elaine Greenberg, Judith Hayashi, Jeannette Hung, James Hunter, Judy Hyashi, Riz Ibrahim, Gillian Johnston, Jim Kelly, Henri Labatt, Bruce Lawson, Donald Lawson, Stephen Lewis, Billy Lowe, Grant Lowry, John Mackenzie, Doug Manning, Pam Pons Marier, Barb Mason, Kevin Maynard, John McCormick, Elizabeth McTavish, Barbara Moses, Bill O'Byrne, Elaine O'Reilly, Vance Peavy, Joan Richardt, Murray Ross, Sue Rossan, Nancy Schaefer, Rob Shea, Russell Sheppard, Cathy Simpson, Jim Simpson, Sherri Simzer, Rob Straby, Dave Studd, Gail Takahashi, Carol Tumber, Pat Warner, Susan Wayne and Bill Wolfson.

A NOTE TO READERS

A Coming of Age: Counselling Canadians for Work in the Twentieth Century is based on transcripts from hundreds of hours of interviews commissioned from career counsellors across Canada. The Coming of Age Advisory Group would like to thank everyone who worked so hard to make this book a reality.

Introduction

In the days approaching the turn of this century, many of us were caught up in the reflective mood sweeping our nation and the nations of the world. This book begins at the turn of the last century, during which you will read how the world of work was forever changed, as were the professions concerned with supporting the Canadian workforce.

In the late fall of 1998, The Counselling Foundation of Canada began to consider ways to celebrate the passage of the Canadian career counselling community into the new millennium. Our reflections on how best to mark the milestones and accomplishments of the community coincided with a recognition of the challenges still to be met. So as we celebrated our fortieth anniversary, The Counselling Foundation of Canada set out to document the historical evolution of the career counselling community in Canada, thus far, and to ascertain from members of the profession what they anticipated the future holds.

We believe a historical snapshot of the career counselling profession is an appropriate celebration of the achievements and the multitude of contributions made by individuals, agencies, organizations and institutions that have, over the last century, created the professional community to which we belong. This history, we have discovered, is peppered with foresight, commitment, collaboration and even some professional competitiveness, all of which fostered innovation. This has fueled recognition of the important role career counsellors play in Canada and abroad.

We secured a number of researchers to work under the guidance of an Advisory Group. They gathered information by reviewing primary documents and interviewing a wide range of people associated with career counselling: from Second World War veterans educated as career counsellors by the federal government through to practitioners and career theorists active in the career counselling community in Canada today. A feedback forum composed of a broadly based group of Canadian career practitioners was held in the fall of 1999. At the Feedback Forum and through written submissions, the information collected was validated, expanded and further clarified. We very much appreciate the time and input those who have participated in this research process provided.

Compiling this book has been no easy task. Career counselling has evolved differently in the communities—whether defined geographically or by special interest—it has served. This project only begins to tell the story of the development of the profession at the most general level. The process of making this book illustrated to us as its commissioners, the diversity of backgrounds, experience and perspective that resides within career counselling today. This is one of the profession's great strengths—but it makes writing an authoritative history of its emergence very challenging. We know we haven't got it all right; but we think the essence of Canadian life, which has so significantly shaped this profession, is accurately depicted, and provides a context through which newcomers to the career development world will better understand the professional history they've inherited. We encourage you over the coming year to help us flesh out the details of how the profession, as you know it, has evolved. We see this book as the beginning of the telling, not the end; as a starting point for us to explore together from where we've come, and begin to imagine where we're going.

We thank Janis Foord Kirk, David Kirk and Kirkfoord Communications, and members of the Advisory Group for their efforts in bringing this project to fruition.

The Counselling Foundation of Canada was created by Frank G. Lawson as a vehicle through which he could direct his personal philanthropy as well as his determination to promote the development of career counselling in Canada. The first evidence of his becoming aware of the need for counselling came through his involvement in the Toronto YMCA under the executive leadership of Taylor Statten, a gentleman who subsequently became one of Canada's leading summer camp leaders. (An article on career counselling written by Taylor Statten and published by the YMCA in 1912 is included on page 17.)

As a prisoner of war for nineteen months in 1917/18, Frank Lawson made extensive use of books that were sent to him and the prison camp library, located in Freiberg University. His reading included research on potential careers, which led him to pursue a career in the financial industry on his return to Canada. He joined a small bond firm to learn that particular business and was loaned by his firm to the Victory Loan Committee, for which he served as assistant secretary in 1919. In the early 1920s, he was seconded from his position in the investment industry to the position of Secretary/Administrator of the Federation for Community Services, the forerunner of the United Way campaigns in Toronto.

His career in the financial industry was primarily as a stockbroker. In 1919, he was a founding member of the Board of Trade Club, a group of young men in business who gathered weekly for fellowship and self-development. Some years later, he was one of three who created the Toronto Junior Board of Trade to provide the next generation of young men with the benefits they enjoyed in the Board of Trade Club. The Toronto Junior Board of Trade became part of the Canadian and International Junior Chamber of Commerce movements. Self-development was a primary aim of these organizations.

Frank Lawson served for many years as a Governor of the Toronto Stock Exchange and was prominent in bringing about the merger of the Toronto Stock Exchange and the Standard Stock and Mining Exchange. He followed this with a term as Chairman of the Building Committee, responsible for the Toronto Stock Exchange building erected on Bay Street in Toronto, and then in 1938 he served as Chairman of the Board of Governors.

Throughout his lifetime, Frank Lawson maintained his association with the YMCA, of which he was a member for over eighty of his ninety-two years. His involvement with Dr. Gerald Cosgrave and the YMCA Counselling Service is outlined in this book. During twenty-five years experience as member and chairman of the Toronto YMCA Counselling Service, Frank Lawson experienced the wide extent of the need for counselling. Over 20,000 persons were counselled by the YMCA service during this period. Most of these persons could be helped best by professional and experienced counsellors. Throughout these years he interviewed and mentored many young men who had used the Counselling

Service. The experience of this service demonstrated that there are individuals who need counselling at every career stage, up to planning for retirement.

In 1955, Frank Lawson retired from leadership of his stock brokerage firm and devoted his attention to making things happen in the field of career counselling. As the demand for counsellors increased across the country, Frank Lawson established The Counselling Foundation of Canada to assist organizations that were doing counselling, as well as help universities broaden their programs to include the training of counselling psychologists. The Counselling Foundation of Canada, chartered in 1959, provided a degree of anonymity for Frank Lawson. He never sought recognition for his efforts or philanthropy, much of the latter being done anonymously. He reluctantly accepted an Honorary Degree from York University because he thought by doing so he would bring recognition to and advance the field of career counselling.

The bulk of Frank G. Lawson's estate was bequeathed to The Counselling Foundation of Canada. With Frank Lawson's death, the nature of the Foundation changed from a personal crusade to a well-endowed foundation whose members include his children and grandchildren. The Foundation is managed by a Board of Directors, which honours Frank Lawson's legacy of service and philanthropy through its adherence to his early goals and commitment. Subsequently one-half of Gerald Cosgrave's estate was also transferred to the capital of the Foundation providing a means of carrying on his legacy to his chosen profession. On behalf of the Directors of The Counselling Foundation of Canada, we dedicate this book to the memory of these two pioneers: Frank G. Lawson and Gerald Cosgrave.

The work of The Counselling Foundation of Canada is carried out by the Executive Director who reviews funding proposals and helps organizations establish and create important programs that relate to counselling. First Elizabeth McTavish, and now Jean Faulds, the Executive Directors of the Foundation have made major contributions to the field of counselling through their efforts of which we are greatly appreciative.

As we bring this phase of the project to a close, we face a changed world in the aftermath of terrorist attacks in North America and renewed hostilities around the world. No doubt this century will continue to bring unimaginable challenges which will, as always, have an impact on the nature of work, and the skills and experience needed by Canadians to fulfill their career needs.

Career counselling remains an integral part of Canadian society, and has certainly come of age.

On behalf of the Board and Members of The Counselling Foundation of Canada,

Donald G. Lawson
Chairman
January, 2002

THE
Century
THAT
Redefined
Work

Never before in the history of humankind has a one-hundred-year period been as eventful as the one just ended. The 20th century will be remembered as the century of World Wars, the automobile, flight, television, man's first steps on the surface of the moon, and the computer. And it began with a fantastic event, Marconi's famous transatlantic wireless message received in St. John's Newfoundland, ushering in a century of remarkable transformations.

In Canada's career counselling community, itself a child of those hundred years, much that happened can be seen as part of its process of maturation. Almost everything that occurred in the 20th century represented a change in the nature of work, whether it was the advent of mass manufacturing, mass communications, information technology or nuclear arms. Whenever something new appeared, it had an impact on jobs—on what people did, and where and how they did it.

As the 19th century drew to a close, Canada remained a vast frontier, home to scarcely more than five million people. Well over half the population still lived in rural areas, while some two million had migrated into a relatively few cities and towns.

National Archives of Canada

1900: Haying in Saskatchewan. Wheat would become Canada's primary export as agriculture continued to grow.

The Canadian workforce consisted of roughly 1.8 million people, the vast majority of whom were men. For most, work was a means of survival and anyone who wanted work could generally find it.

In large part, the work of the era was physical. Manual labour demanded people with strength and stamina who knew how to use their hands. Even the most skilled craftsmen of the day—carpenters, stone masons and blacksmiths—relied on manual abilities.

There was work to be found for saddlers, shoemakers, textile workers and printers. Labourers built sidewalks, roads, bridges and railways.

National Archives of Canada

1910: Immigrants came in the thousands looking for a new productive life in a vast country.

Those willing to venture into the Canadian wilderness found work trapping or in logging and mining camps. In small coastal communities, people fished for a living. And everywhere in the raw, new land, there was farming. As the century began, over 700,000 people worked in some form of agriculture.

The vast expanse of prairie, stretching west across the country, had not yet been settled to any great extent. Aside from the burgeoning port of Vancouver and a few thousand pioneering souls in rough-hewn frontier towns like Calgary, the country was still largely made up of what had been called Upper and Lower Canada, plus the Maritime provinces.

Massive numbers of immigrants poured into Canada each year, often without money, counting on finding work. Many headed west, in search of land, but fully half the new arrivals ended up in Canadian cities, where slum-like areas spread rapidly and health concerns became increasingly common.

In Montreal, Halifax and Toronto, there were cabinet-makers, distillers, wagon and carriage builders. Industrialization, still in its infancy, had nonetheless already begun its transformation of work; the free market economy it encouraged was gathering strength. Many of the early factories were "little more than huge craft shops," observes social historical, Alvin Finkel. "You'd have a lot of people operating their craft, but operating it for an employer."

Career counselling, to the degree that it existed at all, was dispensed by lay persons and social workers in community agencies or church basements. And no one had yet put the words "career" and "counselling" together to describe a process intended to help individuals determine where in the workplace their interests might be best served.

Among the most powerful forces that would promote change throughout the century were the needs for guidance and direction felt by those in Canada's increasingly sprawling, diverse workplace. Changing social, economic and political realities created the need to help young people leaving school or people leaving the farm and moving to cities looking for work; the need to help people acquire new skills to deal with changing technology; and the need to help those new to the county.

From its earliest years, Canada was a country of immigrants. Throughout the century ahead, there would be tremendous pressures on new Canadians to adapt and become productive members of society. People of many nationalities with widely differing backgrounds and skills needed help getting settled, looking for work and finding their way in a strange land.

As the 20th century began, however, there was little recognition of these career and workplace needs, and little expectation among those in need of career counselling that help would be forthcoming.

Then, as now, entrepreneurs flourished. A couple of major Canadian retailers—The T. Eaton Company and Simpson's Ltd.—already had large stores in downtown Toronto and extensive catalogue divisions.

And there were corporate mergers. In 1891, Ontario's Massey Manufacturing Company and A. Harris and Son joined forces to become Massey-Harris, Canada's largest corporation, manufacturer of over half the agricultural machinery sold nationwide.

Throughout the course of the coming century, there would be both good and bad employers and an individual's quality of working life would depend, to a large degree, on which sort one worked for. As well, the needs of employers would change time and again, as market forces transformed the means of production and skill requirements were altered accordingly.

In the early years, most establishments remained small, with fewer than a hundred employees; workers and employers formed personal relationships. As the Industrial Age advanced however, and companies and institutions grew, managers began to represent the employers' interests to the workers.

The roots of career counselling in the community

In those years, many of the sectors that would eventually play a role in responding to workers' needs for direction were busy grappling with their own realities. Governments, for example, were preoccupied with finding ways to build the new nation. Generally they saw the interests of employers as closely linked to their own. Education was largely a local concern. One-room schoolhouses dotted settled areas; larger school boards could only be found in major cities. "By 1905," says Alvin Finkel, "with the exception of Quebec, Canadian provinces had legislated free schooling and compulsory attendance for youngsters under the age of twelve."

Public education, for the most part, was oriented toward building basic skills of reading, writing and arithmetic. Already, however, there were calls from social reformers to include practical instruction on manual training and household science in the schooling of young people. In cities, private training institutes had begun to appear as well, providing clerical training and, in a few trade organizations, technical training.

Craft labour unions provided some help, but only to union members. "The labour movement at the time was really a group of skilled workers," says labour educator D'Arcy Martin. "You had large numbers of street smart, highly skilled workers banding together and negotiating with skills as their main lever; unskilled workers were perceived by these journeymen as the great unwashed."

Only in the community agencies of the day was there much help with employment and training concerns. Organizations like the Salvation Army, the YMCA (Young Men's Christian Association) and the YWCA (Young Women's Christian Association) had set up offices in the country's major cities, offering help finding accommodation, work and, at times, even training to those who came to their doors.

Canada was still a British colony (and Newfoundland an independent colony) and British expatriots and social activists were prominent among those providing assistance. In most communities, there were social workers who gave their time to churches or religious organizations.

For people who found themselves truly destitute, the only refuge was the civic poor house, where "relief" was often dispensed in a parsimonious and begrudging way.

World wars and times of great upheaval

Ahead lay a century of tumultuous change. Wars would both drain the economy and revitalize it. Economic contraction and expansion, industrial growth and decline, consumerism, and astonishing technological advances all would have their impact on the workplace. Canada's colossal geography would demand creative responses in transportation and communications. And somewhere in the distant, unimaginable future, people would be crisscrossing its vast expanse in massive jetliners and eventually conducting "virtual" interactions in cyperspace.

Over and over again, work and its role in society would change, buffeted by market forces, political shifts and international events until, by the end of the 20th century, no corner of the Canadian workplace would be immune... and few workers unaffected.

Career distress, the bane of the low-skilled or disadvantaged, would become commonplace. Displaced workers would need relocation assistance. Unemployed executives would need help learning how to look for work. The long-term unemployed would need motivation and help rebuilding lost self-esteem. New entrepreneurs would require financial support to get started. Young people would need higher education, training and ever more sophisticated skills. And virtually everyone would need better, more comprehensive information and the skills to adapt to an ever-changing job market and workplace.

As the years of the 20th century passed and individual needs grew, society would be pressed to respond. During times of upheaval, there would be calls for sweeping government programs to deal with complex workplace issues creating, by century's end, a huge bureaucracy to help individuals and employers deal with workplace issues.

As early as the middle of the century, some corporate employers would find it in their own best interests to help workers address their personal career counselling needs. By the end of the century, education would advance in unimaginable ways, ultimately becoming part of a global "learning market," offering instruction and training to millions of young people and adults each year.

Even organized labour, while continuing to be concerned with wages, benefits and workplace regulations, would increasingly shift its gaze to the needs of individual members for career guidance and counselling.

New beginnings

Innovation in career and employment services, and the impetus to see them widely adopted across the country would come from individuals working within these various sectors.

Far-sighted business philanthropist Frank Lawson would see the need for vocational guidance and devote his ample energies to meeting that need. Early psychologist Gerald Cosgrave would work diligently to provide people with personal vocational insight.

Clarence Hincks, an inspired social activist, would find his way into schools and corporate boardrooms, galvanizing people to action. Educator Morgan Parmenter would create some of Canada's first labour market information for young people. And public servant Stuart Conger would help to shape the role played by the federal government in developing youthful human capital.

Often working independently and inspired by their own visions, these pioneers and many, many others would find a common cause, ultimately helping to create a field that would benefit the country's capacity to compete globally and meet its own needs. They would contribute to the establishment of a profession of career counselling practitioners, whose role evolved from placement agents supplying the labour needs of a diversifying

Two pioneers
Frank G. Lawson (left)
and Morgan Parmenter

economy, to professionals helping Canadians assess their skills and interests and equipping them to chart their own career path in the new economy.

As work was redefined by the 20th century, so too was a profession that helped Canadians adapt and ensured the economy had a reliably skilled labour supply to meet its needs. *A Coming of Age: Counselling Canadians for Work in the Twentieth Century* provides an overview of Canada's social history, with particular emphasis on work and the economy that supplied it. It provides the context within which career counselling emerged as an inherent part of every working Canadian's life.

CHAPTER 2

THE
Early Years

O n New Year's Eve, 1899, Canada was a nation on the threshold of enormous change. A gold rush was underway in the Klondike and startling new technologies had already begun to revolutionize the world of work. The nation's first hydroelectric plant had opened at Niagara Falls. The first magnetic sound recording had been made. No less than three steel mills were now operational in the land, confirming the nation's arrival in the industrial world. The Bank of Montreal already employed close to six hundred people nationwide. Imperial Oil had opened its headquarters in a parlour-sized upstairs room in Winnipeg.

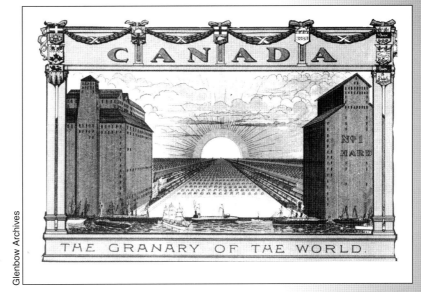

Glenbow Archives

1903: A government publication describes the country's bounty.

In Toronto, several buildings towered over six storeys high. The city's first telephone exchange—serving forty subscribers—had been installed by none other than Alexander Graham Bell. On the streets, horse-drawn trolleys that had lumbered along tracks crisscrossing the city's main thoroughfares were giving way to electrical streetcars that hurtled along at incredible speeds of up to twenty miles an hour. The factories were still powered by steam, gas lamps lit the city streets and Canada was prosperous. A worldwide boom that had started late in the previous century benefited the new nation enormously; prices of raw materials, its main exports, outstripped the prices of manufactured products, its primary imports.

They were heady days. Under the able direction of its first French Canadian prime minister, the federal government addressed itself to nation building. Eloquent and charming, Wilfrid Laurier was a master of political compromise, continuing and expanding upon the National Policy introduced by his predecessor and political foe, John A. Macdonald.

Canada was a society in the midst of transformation, with largely rural roots and new growing shoots of industry. Up to the turn of the century, well over half the population still worked the land and self-employment was implicit in most people's definition of work.

In the political mindset of the day, immigration was seen as the key to growth. Canada had not proven as popular a destination for settlers as the United States however, and the rush of immigrants anticipated by the Fathers of Confederation in 1867 had been slow to arrive.

Then, in 1896, with the closing of American public land, the Canadian prairies became known as the "Last Best West."[1] Clifford Sifton, Laurier's Minister of the Interior, was the architect of a brilliantly successful immigration campaign. Settlers from Britain, Europe and the U.S. poured into the country. In less than fifteen years, Canada became a new home for some two million immigrants. Enticed by Sifton's promises of free land, many of these new arrivals headed west.

The country's economic well-being was vastly increased in these years. Thirty thousand new farms were established each year and national wheat production tripled every five. Wheat became Canada's primary export and shipments increased by a factor of ten.

The young country's new farmers were consumers as well, buying lumber for their homes from one part of the country and nails and glass from another. The economy grew at an unprecedented rate, stirring John Hobson, a political economist visiting from Britain, to declare in 1906 that, "a single decade has swept away all of [Canada's] diffidence, and has replaced it by a spirit of boundless confidence and booming enterprise."[2]

In the flush of its new prosperity, the country's infrastructure expanded steadily. The last spike had been driven on the Canadian Pacific Railway in 1885 but, by the turn of the century, it was clear that a single transcontinental line would not be adequate to the national need, especially for the shipments of grain from the west. New lines were built, providing further links between west and east and, for the first time, pushing toward the northern frontier. In every direction, as the rails advanced, people followed and new industries were created.

Shipping, forestry and mining flourished. Nickel reserves discovered in Sudbury allowed Canada to acquire a near monopoly in global production, while the silver deposits of nearby Cobalt turned out to be the richest in the world. In British Columbia, the fishing industry doubled in size, spawning economic growth throughout the province. And in south-

At the turn of the century, farming was the principal occupation of many Canadians.

National Archives of Canada

ern Ontario, the taming of Niagara Falls provided "white coal"—hydro-electric power—for countless new applications including the smelting of steel in Hamilton, Ontario.

Everywhere Canada's budding entrepreneurs turned, it seemed, the vast land yielded its riches and new work appeared. For all the bounty it offered, however, the land remained a tough taskmaster. Agriculture was still the primary provider and life on the farm and in rural communities was frequently harsh. Farming was a risky business, complicated by unpredictable weather, tariffs, prices that fluctuated on the speculative free market, arbitrary freight rates and the availability of rail transportation to get the crop to port.

Like farmers, the country's trappers and fishermen worked the seasonal cycles of the northern climate, the fruits of their labours often going straight from hand to mouth. Others felled trees or worked in mines or canneries. Still others built roads, towns, cities and railways.

Considerable numbers of new immigrants, especially those without agricultural skills or English language ability, ended up doing the dirtiest and most dangerous work of all. Many joined the pool of mobile labourers known as "bunkhouse men," separated from their families and consigned to dirty shacks, working long hours for meager wages in mining, harvesting, construction and logging.

The work of that frontier era was generally gruelling, sometimes dangerous and frequently poorly paid. Only an elite few had what we think of today as a career, enjoying the luxury of any personal choice in how they were to earn a living. Some families produced politicians and diplomats, as well as professionals, clergy and soldiers, but the majority of people still won their living with their hands. Brawn, muscle and a strong back were the work skills most in demand.

In the more settled areas of the country—in central Canada and to a lesser degree in Nova Scotia and New Brunswick—industrialization, and the free market economy it encouraged, gathered strength. As manufacturing production lines became increasingly common, notably in Ontario and Quebec, the nature of work continued to change.

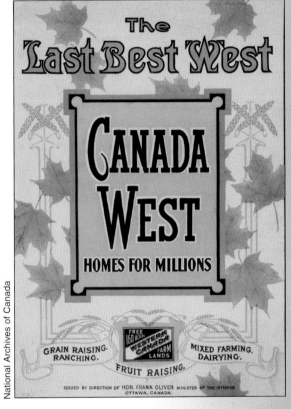

Canada was successfully promoted as the "Last Best West" to settlers from Britain, Europe and the U.S.

Migration to the towns and cities

Drawn by the new opportunities, people from the countryside began to move into the growing towns and cities to work in factories, stores and offices. For these people, Canada's early working class, notions of self-sufficiency began to give way to another way of making a living—the so-called "steady job."

The urban centres grew rapidly. During the first two decades of the century, Vancouver's population increased fivefold. Towns like Calgary, Edmonton, Saskatoon and Regina sprang up on the sites of former trading posts and small settlements. Toronto and Montreal, already Canada's largest cities, doubled in size.[3] By 1911, Quebec and Ontario had the largest urban concentrations.

Growth of this kind was largely unregulated however, and civic gov-

1910: Immigrant families arrive at Toronto's Union Station carrying their belongings in make-shift bundles.

1911: A father and his sons arrive in Toronto from Britain to begin their new life in Ontario.

Circa 1900: Thousands of immigrants from many countries flocked to Canada including these outside the Dominion Government Immigration Hall in Winnipeg.

ernments were challenged to meet the demands of the many social problems it created. On one side of town, affluent city dwellers lived a good, sometimes opulent, life, while on the other, ghetto-like slums grew quickly. Class and ethnic divisions divided people. Sanitation was a problem, water was unsafe to drink and infant mortality rates were high.

In the jostle and shove of these competitive hubs, skilled craftspeople enjoyed a higher status among workers, protected by their unions. But as the century progressed, traditional craft shops continued to lose ground to the burgeoning factory system. Investing their faith in the efficient techniques of mass manufacturing, factory employers systematically reduced the available work to its smallest components, simplifying tasks so that only low-level skills were required. In this manner, employers fought for and imposed a low-wage system, managing their workers according to the profit-and-loss arithmetic of the industrial era, ensuring that costs remained low and production levels high. And steadily, inexorably, independent and skilled craftspeople were replaced by unskilled labourers who were treated as commodities, ledger entries, "units of production."

As ever greater numbers of people began to exchange their labour for wages, working relationships became more and more impersonal. The managers who ran the company towns, the logging, mining and construction camps, and the coastal fisheries and canneries, imposed strict supervision and production quotas.

People were overworked and labour undervalued. It was a rough and tumble world of sweatshops, poor working conditions and exploitation.

But whatever they did, and wherever they found themselves in the workforce, people needed help to find and keep employment. They needed language skills, agricultural skills and technical skills. They needed direction. And they needed guidance to understand how to function and adapt to a new country and an emerging workplace.

> "Their expectations were low, revolving around work and survival. Indeed, they were preoccupied with survival… they were willing to work long hours and endure much discomfort if it allowed them security and a viable future for their offspring."
>
> Jaroslav Petryshyn,
> *Peasants in the Promised Land,*
> *Canada and the Ukrainians*
> *1891-1914*

Community responses to workers' needs

The laissez-faire philosophy espoused by Laurier's government held that the nation's economic well-being was the responsibility not of bureaucrats but of the marketplace. Relationships between employers and employees were all but unregulated and, in the mood of nation building that gripped the government, few restrictions were placed on businesses. The needs of the poor and unemployed were left largely to charity. Church workers and volunteers affiliated with settlement houses and charitable organizations offered what assistance they could.

Catholic organizations such as the St. Vincent de Paul, the Benevolent Irish Societies and the Grey Nuns had a long history of providing services to destitute Catholics. Among Protestant organizations, the first Canadian YMCA had made its appearance in Montreal in 1851. By 1900, YMCAs and YWCAs existed in other major centres, including Toronto, Hamilton and Vancouver. The urban unemployed and poor relied heavily on assistance from organizations such as these.

Then, as now, it was understood that personal and working success were inseparably intertwined. And in the not-for-profit sector, with its focus on helping people develop their potential, some form of vocational guidance was seen as essential. There were, of course, no aptitude tests, motivational videos, practice interviews or self-evaluation exercises. But by the turn of the century, the YMCA and YWCA offered training and placement services for men and women. And in 1910, a YWCA Employment Bureau in Vancouver had nearly three thousand job orders from employers and ultimately placed more than one thousand women in jobs.

Amid the din of urban expansion, massive immigration and advancing industrialization, a frontier mentality held that it was "every man for himself." As for women, they were expected to be in the labour force only when they were single. That being said, some workers' unions were vying for position, the collective voice being recognized as more than that of the individual. Compared with the powerful labour movements that had flourished in Europe however, Canada was considered a backwater when it came to union activity.[4]

The union membership that did exist was largely male, white, Anglo-Saxon and skilled. And many of the people most in need of protection—migrant workers on construction sites, in canneries, in mines or on railway maintenance crews—remained outside the labour movement's influence or concern.

More than half the unionized workers in Canada at the turn of the century were affiliated with the American Federation of Labor, which dominated the Canadian labour scene at the time. Skilled labour moved back and forth across the Canadian-American boundary in all regions. As workers moved from place to place in search of work, with little regard for borders, they depended on their international craft unions to protect their rights.

In the early days of the century, organized labour was effective at calling strikes and workplace disputes were common in a range of industries such as coal mining, cotton processing, communications and railways. When push came to shove, however, little was accomplished, at least from the perspective of workers. Governments often intervened on the side of employers, even to the extent of calling in the militia to force people back to work.

1912: Child labour was accepted, even in the coal mines.

National Archives of Canada

Capitalist exploitation spawned a new breed of labour leader committed to fight for the rights of industrial age workers. R. B. (Bob) Russell was one such leader. A Scot, Russell worked as a machinist for one of the country's largest employers, the CPR (Canadian Pacific Railway). An early champion of "One Big Union," he went on to run for the Independent Labour Party in Assiniboia, Manitoba.

In his column in *The Machinists Bulletin*, Russell wrote, "The days of the craft unions are over. The call of the working class for Industrial Union has gone out in order to meet the great change in Industrial Expansion and construction of the new machinery."

The social reform movement

"Though many will tell you that times are bad, there are now, as always, a certain number of employers looking for workers, and men out of employment seeking work. What can be simpler than to bring them together?"

The year was 1914. The place was Montreal. And the workplace crusader posing the question was Etta St. John Wileman, British expatriate and member of the staunchly conservative and Protestant Imperial Federation League.

Carried in the wake of the waves of British and U.S. immigrants arriving on Canadian shores was an active social reform movement, closely connected with major Protestant churches. Although at times high-minded and patronizing in their views, these reformers lobbied governments for better housing, recreational and health facilities, better sewers and sanitation.

After years of growth, Canada's economy was in the doldrums. Overseas investment had fallen off badly. Urban unemployment had climbed to an estimated 25 percent. To social activists like Miss Wileman, the lack of meaningful government action was intolerable. "What is wrong with the brains of the nation," she railed, "that the labour market is unorganized resulting in idleness and distress?"[5]

Her concerns were well-founded, though they might not have found their mark had it not been for the march of events. A world war had just begun and Canada was committed to play its part. The national job market was already flooded with an excess of workers, but immigrants from Britain, Europe and the United States continued to pour into the country in search of new opportunities, unaware of the strain they were adding to an already difficult situation.

Wileman's vision was clear and uncompromising. For a couple of years, she had been seeking support across Canada, canvassing politicians and business leaders, asking them to "recognize their responsibility for the unemployed. Work," she declared, was "a social obligation, which has to be provided in order that both individual and state may reap the benefit of constant regular productivity."[6]

> "The true makers of Canada were those who, in obscurity and poverty, made it with axe and spade, with plough and scythe, with sweat of face and strength of arm."
>
> Robert Sellar, 1915

The need for some form of assistance for individuals in finding and retaining productive work had been obvious to reformers for decades. Employment, jobs and the very meaning of work were changing and people were hard-pressed to keep up. Arguments such as Wileman's, however, ran into the ingrained view that a man who really wanted to find work could always do so. And the limited social assistance available to able-bodied unemployed men at the time reflected this deeply held prejudice. In Ontario, before they could receive food and shelter in a "house of industry," as workhouses were called, unemployed single men had to perform a work test such as breaking rocks. In New Brunswick and Nova Scotia, entire families were forced into workhouses since provincial authorities would not accept that a man could not find work and they would not provide assistance to an unemployed man and his family unless they all agreed to enter the workhouse.

Amid the angst and uncertainty of those turbulent years, on the cusp of an agricultural economy and an industrial age, there was precious little help for the unemployed. There were few records of the labour market, no analyses of industries and wages, no official statistics. People trying to find their way in the new country's frontier workplace had few services to guide them. Recent immigrants had little help finding their way into the workplace. No one had counsellors to help them find the work best suited to them. In fact, a Royal Commission investigating the practises of employment agencies in Montreal found that Italian immigrant labourers were often exploited. The Commission recommended the strict licensing of labour bureaus to regulate the recruitment of immigrants.[7]

In a few of the larger cities, some craft unions ran non-profit employment offices, but only for union members. The so-called "labour agents" and commercial employment agencies of the day worked exclusively on behalf of employers, often at the expense of the individuals they recruited.

The needs of the economy were paramount.

Labour and legislation

Collective organization was somewhat more successful on the prairies than in other regions. Early in the century, Canadian farmers had banded together to lobby the government for better freight rates and the elimination of tariffs. Over the years, cooperative grain growers' associations had become a strong collective voice for western farmers.

1908: Women work alongside men in factories.

There had been occasional earlier attempts to protect workers' rights, among them the federal Conciliation Act, which made its debut along with a brand new Department of Labour in 1900. In 1907, as the first McLaughlin motor car came off the line in Oshawa and the country's first service station opened in Vancouver, Canada's first significant piece of labour legislation was passed. Written by William Lyon Mackenzie King, the Industrial Disputes Investigation Act would define labour relations in Canada for decades to come. Intended to be fair to both sides, the purpose of the legislation was to prevent industrial conflict from deterring economic growth. It provided for a cooling-off period and conciliation proceedings as the best methods of encouraging industrial peace. But many employers used the no-strike period to build up inventory and locate replacement employees. Passing laws was no solution in itself. Given the inadequate inspection services of the day, applying them was something else again.

An economic downturn in 1907 threw thousands of people out of work. The country slumped into a deep but brief recession. Over the next year or so factories closed, construction ground to a halt and the number of urban unemployed grew. There was little work in rural areas either and, as large numbers of people migrated into Canadian cities, the load was more than the private employment agencies could handle.

City of Toronto Archives

A role for government

Some of the provinces began to address the unemployment problem. Ontario opened a government labour employment bureau in Hamilton and another in Ottawa to place urban workers in jobs. A year later, Quebec followed suit, creating a system of government employment offices, the most advanced in the country at the time. Civic politicians and administrators began to take an active interest in addressing the needs of the employment market. In a few urban centres, municipal labour bureaus were set up and the unemployed were registered and put to work temporarily for the cities. When the economy improved, however, these municipal offices were shut down.

For the most part, people looking for work were on their own. New immigrants, people moving out of rural areas into cities and young people entering the workforce for the first time all found work in the same way: through newspaper advertisements, commercial agencies, charitable organizations and, sometimes, by sheer luck.

None of these methods was adequate, said Etta St. John Wileman who had begun her crusade for a system of federal employment bureaus in 1912, badgering Calgary's city council into creating a civic employment office and making her the manager. Wileman and her compatriots in the Imperial Federation League may have looked upon Canada with a certain blue blood condescension, but her concern for the worker was genuine.

The federal government's involvement in employment bureaus was essential, she believed, to facilitate the movement of people across the country and to create a trustworthy way to help employers and employees find each other. In true imperialist fervour, she lobbied to link Canadian employment bureaus with the Labour Bureaus established in Britain a few years earlier. British workers wishing to immigrate could register in Britain for job placement in Canada, she proposed.

The need for employment assistance was a "crying necessity," Wileman believed. "We find honest, intelligent men and women giving way to apathy and despair in the constantly recurring struggle of hunting for jobs. And we see children, new to the game of finding work, thrown onto their own resources."[8]

However sincere her pleas, the federal government found reasons to resist them, for a time. Organized labour was not exactly sold on the idea either. Labour leaders tended to oppose federal involvement of this kind, concerned that Ottawa would use the service, as commercial agencies had, to move immigrant workers into areas of labour dispute. Employers, for their part, worried that employment bureaus would interfere with the free movement of workers between the provinces.[9]

Introduction of career guidance

But Etta St. John Wileman's vision reached far beyond the establishment of a national system of employment offices. In her thoughtful and passionate speeches, Wileman lobbied for what is today known as career guidance and counselling in schools and for the publication of labour market information. "What sustained coordinated effort is made throughout the Dominion to ascertain the abilities and natural bent of the child to fit for occupation after school?" she demanded to know. "What knowledge do parents secure as to conditions of trades and occupations, rates of pay, training necessary to give a child a fair start in the Industrial World?"

In the early days of the century, many Canadian students learned their three Rs in a single-room schoolhouse, moving in and out of classes in tandem with family needs. Academic training, if and when it happened, was not necessarily tied to a diploma. In many families, formal education simply wasn't considered a priority, even though compulsory schooling to age fourteen or fifteen was the law in all provinces except Quebec.

In agricultural communities, for the most part, work was a family affair; children attended school only when they weren't needed at home on the farm. In communities where mining, logging, fishing or industry, as the century progressed, created jobs, boys were often required to meet family needs and leave school early to look for work.

When a young person did manage to finish school, and began to think about his or her future, career guidance or counselling was unlikely to be much more than a conversation with the teacher after class as she cleaned the blackboard. If the student was bright and the family could afford it, that discussion might focus on which university the student should consider. But as late as the 1930s, only 1 percent of school children was university-bound. Often the family wasn't up to the costs of higher education or the student's academic skills weren't seen to be strong enough, or both. The teacher's questions would most likely be: "Won't your family need you on the farm?" or "What about talking to the blacksmith in town?" or "How about that new hotel they're building in the next county? Maybe they'll need help."

Higher education resists vocational role

1907: Workers study in a Frontier College classroom. "Education must be obtainable on the farm, in the bush, on the railway and in the mine," said college founder Rev. Alfred Fitzpatrick.

National Archives of Canada

Advanced education had been available in Upper Canada as early as the mid-17th century, but in New France, as it was then called, unless you were a male and destined for a profession or the clergy, it simply wasn't open to you. In the period after the British conquest, a number of universities were gradually established, including Dalhousie University in Halifax in 1818, McGill University in Montreal in 1821, and the University of Toronto in 1827. From then until the middle of the 20th century, Canadian universities—in English Canada, at least—were fashioned on their British counterparts, which were class-conscious and conservative.

Well into the 20th century, university remained a privileged environment largely reserved for white Anglo-Saxon males. Most univer-sity students were the children of the upper and middle classes, bound for specific professional careers: academia, law and engineering.

In Canada's institutions of higher learning there was little require-ment for, or interest, in career or vocational guidance. Educators in these institutions held to the ideal of "pure education" which imparted the fundamentals of traditional European schools of thought with little consideration of workplace applications.

An early and notable exception to this traditional and rather elitist view of education was Frontier College. Founded in 1899 by Rev. Alfred Fitzpatrick, the college's original aim was to "make education available to all." Frontier College "worker-teachers" were sent out across the country, even into remote workplaces, to work side by side with workers and to go into their homes to teach English and help people build some of the skills they needed. "Education must be obtainable on the farm, in the bush, on the railway and in the mine," Fitzpatrick believed. "We must educate the whole family wherever they earn their living: teaching them how to earn and, at the same time, how to grow physically, intellectually and spiritually…This is the real education."

The advent of vocational guidance

The early roots of career and vocational guidance can be found in technical and vocational education. Although the Industrial Revolution didn't gather steam in Canada until after the First World War, south of the border it had been reshaping the workscape as early as the 1870s.

Still, it was not until 1909, when reform activist Frank Parsons' theories were first used in a Vocations Bureau in Boston, that vocational guidance was defined in a clear and concrete way. Early vocational guidance offered in schools tended to rely on Parsons' model and, as the years progressed, was augmented by psychometric assessment and tools.

It was Parsons who identified vocational counselling as consisting of three distinct stages. The first stage, he said, was devoted to gaining a full understanding of oneself. The second was centred on the acquisition of a firm base of knowledge about the workplace and the jobs available. And the third stage concentrated on forming a clear mental image of how to bring the two together.

Vocational guidance evolved slowly in Canadian schools largely because education in Canada falls under provincial government jurisdiction, and each provincial department of education has its own way of doing things. In those days, vocational guidance was targeted almost exclusively to students in technical schools and to the skills and abilities they were going to need in the sort of work they were likely to do. The inclusion of personal, social and psychological factors would have to wait until later in the century.

Vocational training in Canada can be traced back to the middle of the 17th century, when artisans and teachers from France were brought to Quebec to teach rug making. And since the beginning of the 19th century, some kind of vocational training has been available in most regions of the country. Legislation governing training of this kind didn't appear until the early 20th century.

Alongside general training to impart mechanical,

In the early years of the century, few thought about assisting others in their choice of vocation, however here and there voices were echoing the sentiments of Etta St. John Wileman. Commenting on the work of Frank Parsons of the Boston Vocational Bureau, Taylor Statten, the Boys' Work Secretary for the national YMCA offered this advice:

- Consider what you are best fitted for; ask your parents, teachers and friends what they think.
- Study the men who are in the occupations that you wish to enter.
- Do not let your fascination for a career interfere with your serious consideration as to whether or not you are adapted to that work.
- Do not make your inability to decide on a vocation an excuse for idleness, but go ahead and do something at once. More is learned by action than by reflection.
- Do not wander from one job to another. Stick to your work until you are sure you are getting into something better.
- A good training for any one trade will always contain many elements that are applicable to another trade.
- Do not be discouraged if you do not find your vocation early in life. Many men made false starts, and not until later find their real sphere.

From the YMCA's publication, *The Triangle*, January 1912.

1914: William Lyon Mackenzie King — a little-known labour expert — became Canada's labour minister.

1913: Recent immigrants wait to enter one of Winnipeg's eighteen private employment offices, where they hope to find work.

industrial, clerical and domestic skills, the training provided generally reflected the sort of work available in the region. In Newfoundland, for example, young people were taught navigation and net making. Navigation skills were also taught in Nova Scotia, as were mining techniques. Agricultural skills were taught in most provinces.

Although education was a matter of provincial jurisdiction, the federal government became involved in addressing the need of an industrializing economy for skilled workers. There was the perception that labour shortages could critically stall industrial development, which at the time was seen to be at the top of the list of what was "in the national interest."

Ottawa's interest in Canada's vocational educational system began ten years into the 20th century, when the federal government appointed a Royal Commission on Industrial Training and Technical Education. Some of the commission's recommendations were never implemented: it advised that a federal Ministry of Vocational Education be established, for example. The commission had also criticized Canadian education. Established by William Lyon Mackenzie King, who, at the time, was Deputy Minister of Labour, the commission had traveled to each of the provinces, to the United States, the United Kingdom and to Europe, and had returned home with a blunt assessment: "Canada is behind the times."[9]

Canadian education was too "bookish" and not related to "industrial, agricultural or housekeeping life," the commission's report stated. Federal involvement in vocational education and training was necessary because, as the commission pointed out, it was a federal responsibility to provide Canada, as an industrial nation, with an adequate supply of skilled workers.[10]

During the war, many of the country's existing technical and vocational institutions had been conscripted by the federal government to train both military and civilian personnel. Immediately after the conflict, these institutions were returned to the provinces. Nonetheless, the federal government had, for a time, been directly involved in the technical training of adults.

The recommendation that the federal government provide funds to the provinces to encourage vocational education did find its way into federal legislation. In 1913, the federal government passed the Agricultural Instruction Act detailing the ways in which it intended to support provincial vocational training initiatives. Ottawa stipulated the amount of money available and, to some degree, how it should be spent. In a portent of future federal/provincial collaboration, it also mandated a couple of federal initiatives: a publication initiated in Ottawa would be distributed free to interested parties; and an annual conference in the nation's capital would bring provincial and federal officials together.

For the most part, the provinces welcomed the money, though they jealously guarded their right to spend it as they saw fit and challenged the federal government's right to tie conditions to educational funds, determined to protect their educational "turf" as a provincial responsibility.

For technical and vocational students in schools, the little counselling that was available tended to focus on the needs of the workplace, not the individual. Virtually nowhere in Canada or the U.S. did schools offer instruction or guidance on the best methods for students to examine their own strengths, weaknesses, likes and dislikes, or come to a decision about the line of work to which they might be best suited.

War, peace and a dream come true

High levels of unemployment during the recession of 1913 compounded the turmoil that characterized Canada's unregulated labour market and increased the demand for a nationally organized service to match employers and employees. On the prairies, in 1913 and again in 1914, the crops failed. More agricultural workers migrated to the cities, and the numbers of jobless people haunting the streets of Canada's urban centres swelled.

National Archives of Canada

1917: A woman makes fuses in a munitions factory.

Laurier's Liberal government had been defeated in 1911 by Robert Borden's Conservatives. Now, as unemployment increased across the country and people became desperate for work, Borden's government found it could no longer claim that unemployment was not a national issue. Searching for solutions, Ottawa began to take more seriously the pleas of Etta St. John Wileman.

Then, in August 1914, the world went to war. Young Canadian men, many of them out of work and hungry, enlisted, and Canadian charities and volunteers began looking for ways to demonstrate their patriotism. The Great War became a watershed event in Canada, a catalyst for rapid industrial and factory growth. An Imperial Munitions Board was established, fuelling growth in the country's industrial infrastructure. And Canadian factories began producing ships, chemicals, aircraft and explosives.

Wileman stepped up her lobbying efforts, adding a new and persuasive plank to her platform. A federal system was essential, she said, not only to move immigrants to the areas of the country in which their labour was needed, but also to move workers to factories to support the war effort. And once the war had ended, she pointed out, the employment bureaus could help returning veterans and out-of-work munitions factory workers re-establish themselves.

Eventually, doubtless guided by their own self-interests, some senators, provincial premiers and even labour leaders began to climb onto Wileman's bandwagon. Wartime labour radicalism and the apparent popularity among western Canadian workers of Russia's Bolshevik revolution in 1917 had alarmed the traditional elite. They feared that as veterans left military jobs and war industries closed, the unemployed of the nation would pose a threat to political and economic stability.

With the management of Canada's available manpower posing an immediate challenge, the Borden government tentatively began to develop a manpower policy. Compulsory registration of the labour force was mandated. And in the summer of 1918, federal workers won the right to bargain collectively, although strikes and lockouts were banned

City of Toronto Archives

1918: On Armistice Day, the celebration of victory over Germany spills over into the streets of downtown Toronto.

Later that year, after lengthy negotiations with the provinces, and just a week after the November 11 armistice, provincial and federal officials met to work out the details of a national employment service. A month later, as 1918 drew to a close, Borden's cabinet, through an order-in-council, created the Employment Service Council of Canada.

Propelled by a sense of urgency and in the first post-war example of "co-operative federalism," Canada began its initial experiment in the management of its manpower resources. On November 25, 1918, the *Montreal Gazette* carried the headline: "New National System of Employment Office."

"By this plan," the article went on, "the Dominion of Canada will have always at hand accurate information as to the demand and supply of labour in all parts of the country, the extent to which private industry is absorbing the returned soldier and demobilized war workers, the volume of public employment that must be provided to take away any surplus and the localities and trades in which such employment is required."

One big part of Etta St. John Wileman's dream had come true. But the pronounced and growing need for career and employment assistance throughout the rapidly changing workplace had only begun to be met.

[1] Desmond Morton, *A Short History of Canada* (Toronto: McClelland & Stewart, 1992).
[2] Craig Brown, ed, *History of Canada* (Toronto: Key Porter, 2000).
[3] Ibid.
[4] Desmond Morton, *A Short History of Canada* (Toronto: McClelland & Stewart, 1992).
[5] Etta St. John Wileman, *Government Labour Bureaux: Their Scope and Aims* (Montreal: Mercantile Print).
[6] Ibid.
[7] Canadian Encyclopedia (Toronto: McClelland & Stewart).
[8] *The Archivist* - Jan/Feb '89.
[9] John Hunter, *The Employment Challenge* (Ottawa: Government of Canada).
[10] Darius Young, *Historical Survey of Vocational Education in Canada* (North York: Captus Press).

CHAPTER 3

Growth, Decline AND Upheaval

November 11, 1918. Victory should have been sweeter. For four years, the big guns had hammered away in Europe. The youthful Dominion of Canada had acquitted herself nobly, sustaining enormous casualties and earning a reputation among friend and foe as a force to be respected and feared. Now it was over. The "Hun" had been vanquished. The Allies had prevailed. But oh, the cost.

As the Great War ended and the weary survivors headed home, Canadians struggled to comprehend the numbers: 60,661 of their youngest and strongest killed in action; another 172,000 wounded, many severely. For a country of barely eight million people, it was no small sacrifice.

Even the able-bodied had sustained their share of wounds. The bloody years in the trenches had been filled with mind-numbing horror. With help, as well as considerable time and effort, most of the hundreds of thousands of returning veterans would eventually re-establish themselves. But their lives would never be the same.

Within months of the armistice, as if to add insult to injury, a flu epidemic began to circle the globe. Carried by soldiers returning to their homes throughout the British Empire, the virus took millions upon millions of lives worldwide, as many as 50,000 of them in Canada. The war

The City of Toronto Archives

1919: Families are reunited with their loved ones as troops return home, lucky to have survived a bloody war.

may have been over, but the shadow of death still loomed.

And then there was the plight of Canada's working people. Organized labour had emerged from the war stronger, its membership having more than tripled in the space of four years. It was also bitterly resentful. During the war, across the country, workers had sacrificed, motivated by official rhetoric about the war leading to a better world. Now they wanted their rewards. Little was forthcoming.

The fruits of the war had gone largely to a select few—businessmen and speculators mostly—who had earned huge profits from war contracts. Little of this windfall had found its way into the pockets of workers. Wages might have increased on paper, but inflation running as high as 54 percent, had cancelled out any actual gains. Nor had there been a legitimate way to protest the inequities. Legislation of 1918 had given some workers the right to organize and bargain collectively but, for the duration of the war, strikes had been banned.

> "Grass will grow, the river will reach the sea, the boy will become a man, and labour will come into its own."
>
> Fred J. Dixon, 1919,
> one of the leaders of the Winnipeg Strike.

The only profit for most Canadians was measured in vague feelings of national pride. The obscure colony in the west with its hodgepodge collection of regions and nationalities had acquired—with the significant exception of francophone Quebec—a new, unified identity. As one Canadian veteran put it, "We went up Vimy Ridge as Albertans and Nova Scotians. We came down as Canadians."

Beyond the valour of her soldiers, Canada's shift in stature abroad was due in no small part to her prime minister. It was Robert Borden's insistence, during the war and following it, that Canada and other British Dominions be treated as sovereign powers. Borden was present at the Paris Peace Conference in 1919 and Canada signed the Treaty of Versailles in her own right.

The nation's economic prospects had been greatly enhanced by the war. The export market for Canadian products had surged. British munitions orders had created a billion dollar manufacturing boom. And the working population, which now included some thirty thousand women who had been mobilized to join the civilian workforce, was far better skilled.

There was more than enough fuel in place, in other words, to fire the economy, had Ottawa's management of the situation been more competent. Instead, the Union government Borden had forged as a way to sell conscription to the country found itself overwhelmed by massive reconstruction problems. Borden lingered overseas even after the peace treaty had been signed and there was a general resentment among his colleagues about his absence when there were so many domestic problems demanding attention.

Post-war employment downturns

Immediately following the armistice, Canada's munitions factories were closed and put up for sale, leaving two hundred thousand or so workers to join the rest of the unemployed. Some of the half million returning soldiers managed to find their way into jobs. Often they replaced women who had taken on the better paying jobs during

1919: Just after the war, unemployment is high and people are desperate to find jobs. Reading the want ads is a daily occupation.

wartime but who were now expected to give them up to make room for returning soldiers. Thousands upon thousands of men failed to find work, however, and the large numbers of displaced soldiers hanging about at loose ends exacerbated the mood of growing social unrest.

As crisis after crisis hit the country, there was a tremendous need for a strong hand at the helm to manage the transition from war to peace. For the most part, the government's pre-war laissez-faire attitude prevailed, however the government did create a Department of Soldiers Civil Re-establishment and, in 1919, a new federal Department of Health.

The help available couldn't begin to meet the need, however. Re-establishment land grants and pensions were only offered to veterans who weren't able to work. And although the new national system of Employment Bureaus matched some workers with jobs, there was little assistance for those who were unsuccessful in their search.

Frustrated by the apparent indifference of the government that had courted them so assiduously to meet their wartime "manpower quotas," veterans' groups organized. They believed they hadn't been adequately compensated for the years in which they had earned about $1.10 a day. Some 250,000 veterans and their supporters demanded a "re-establishment bonus" of $2,000, suggesting that the businessmen who had so richly profited from the war should pay for it.

Not surprisingly, business resisted the idea. And upon learning that the price tag for such a scheme would be one billion dollars, federal politicians and even some of the veterans' leaders followed suit. Ultimately, the veterans' voices fell silent. The government took the opportunity to trim back even further on its previous offerings.[1]

Workers unite

Some veterans, however, linked up with a force that was far less docile: Canada's workers. Their built-up frustration found an outlet in May, 1919. Reacting to a dispute over wages and collective bargaining rights in the building and metal trades, the Winnipeg Trades and Labour Council called a general strike and thirty thousand workers from fifty different unions walked out. Countless businesses from manufacturing companies to restaurants were affected and the city was all but shut down.

The unrest spread quickly, as sympathy strikes sprang up in Toronto, Vancouver, Edmonton and Calgary. In consultation with provincial and federal officials, Winnipeg's business and civic leaders feared that labour was staging a Bolshevik-like revolution. A Citizens' Committee was formed, with a mandate to break the strike. A force of "special police" was established to replace regular police officers, who were themselves unionized.

Civic officials, convinced that they were dealing with "enemy alien,"[2] arrested the strike's leaders. They also banned the frequent parades and demonstrations led by pro-strike veterans who denounced politicians and businessmen unwilling to create lasting jobs with decent pay.

On June 21, 1919, or "Bloody Saturday" as it came to be known, workers and labour supporters defied the ban on public meetings and gathered at Winnipeg's market square to protest the arrests. Mounted police, assisted by the special forces armed with clubs, beat back the crowd. Thirty-four were injured, two killed.

It was a classic moment in Canadian workforce history: the key agencies of power were squared off against the discontented mob. For Canada's fledgling industrial union movement, it was a decisive blow from a united front of unenlightened employers and unyielding governments.

Employers were focused on the full "utilization of manpower" at the lowest possible cost and resolute in their opposition to any action that interrupted production. Craft-based unions were threatened that their position in the workplace was being undermined by the unskilled. Governments, for their part, tended to view industrial unions as a communist threat. Nor was the upstart industrial labour movement adequately prepared to assert itself. Its various different organizations were fragmented and often bitterly divided. Its needs were not always clearly articulated.

There's little question that all parties involved had their own compelling reasons for reacting as they did. It is conceivable, however, that insightful and visionary leadership from any of these factions at this critical moment might have initiated some form of creative response and seen through the clamour of protest, recognizing the validity of the need at its core.

Bloody Saturday
June 21, 1919:
Workers and labour
supporters defy a
ban on public
meetings and gather
at Winnipeg's City
Hall to protest the
arrests of labour
leaders. Mounted
police, assisted by
special forces
armed with clubs,
beat back the
crowd. Thirty-four
are injured, two
killed. It was a
galvanizing moment
in Canadian political
history.

The pent-up frustration of the workers had spilled out, and the best response of the powers assembled was to protect their vested interests. To fit comfortably into the dramatically changed post-war workplace, workers needed certain things: a strong collective voice in their negotiations with employers; better working conditions; and more consideration of their concerns in the workplace.

They received none. Instead, in an atmosphere of alarmist and even prejudicial hysteria, business, government and labour defined their interests narrowly in terms of short-term objectives. And the moment was lost.

A resurgent economy: The country's only priority

Ironically, at that time the "non-interventionist" federal government was exploring a wide range of rather visionary labour market policies. The new Employment Service of Canada for which Etta St. John Wileman had campaigned so tirelessly had been established a year earlier. The service's first director, Bryce Stewart, was an economist and teacher with a comprehensive vision of how an employment service could support the labour force, including Unemployment Insurance. Had policies like these been in effect at the time, they might have gone some distance to stem the tide of opposition. But the wheels of change move slowly and it would be years before Stewart's vision crystallized into comprehensive government action.

BRYCE STEWART

"Some of you will smile at all this," said the young economist, as he faced a skeptical audience of municipal authorities. The year was 1916. And Bryce Stewart was a public servant working in Canada's infant Ministry of Labour.

Many of the people listening may well have been amused by Stewart's zealous and optimistic view of the role government could play in the labour market. A considerable number of his suggestions would soon be enshrined in employment policy nonetheless, although it would be more than sixty years before the full sweep of his vision would be realized.

Like Etta St. John Wileman, Bryce Stewart had become convinced that the solution to Canada's employment problems was a nation-wide linkage of free labour exchanges. Not only would these offices match workers with jobs, said Stewart, they would also ensure an appropriate distribution of labour and attempt to match individuals with the jobs most suited to them.

In an era in which labour was viewed in official circles as "manpower" to be effectively utilized, Stewart recognized the importance of developing what would later be called human capital. A practical visionary, he saw labour as an essential component in the creation of the nation's wealth. Like Mackenzie King, Stewart believed that labour was composed of individuals, most of whom needed help if they were to become, not just employed, but employed at work which suited them and for which there was demand.

This was radical thinking in the early part of the century.

Born in 1883 near Brockville, Ontario, Stewart began his career as a schoolteacher. He had gained a sharp sense of the futility felt by the typical fourteen-year-old who left school with no particular skills, no sense of the sort of work to which he might best turn his hand, and an overall

Ultimately it was business, more than any other sector, which got what it wanted in post-war Canada. Tariffs were safeguarded, government controls were loosened and the rampant inflation that had characterized the final years of the war was brought under control. Interest rates rose dramatically, of course, as banks moved against inflation. Speculative trading activity on the Montreal Exchange more than tripled in a year.

In terms of Canada's export trade, most parts of the country had benefited from wartime demand. Agricultural goods and natural resources remained the country's main exports. But in central and eastern Canada, the manufacturing sector had gathered strength as new products like pulp and paper, farm machinery, lumber, rolling mills and steel furnaces had all found markets outside of Canadian borders.

When it came to employee relations, factory owners and managers in industry remained as hard-nosed as ever. The business philosophy of "scientific management" put forward by one of America's first management consultants, Frederick Winslow Taylor, had captured the imagination of industrial capitalists around the world. "Taylorism," as it became known, was a highly logical but rather harsh workplace discipline that valued productivity above humanity or ethics.

Like the character in Charlie Chaplin's classic film *Modern Times*, individual workers were seen as little more than cogs in the wheel. And the industrial employers of the day had the luxury of believing that their interests and the interests of their workers were two separate things.

sense of futility. "He commands only a casual labourer's wage," said Stewart, and at the age of twenty, "is no better equipped than when he entered the work world at fourteen."

Government could play a vital role in helping to shape the working lives of such people, Stewart believed. A trained economist, he saw the situation not merely in terms of the difficulties faced by unguided and untrained workers but also in terms of what this pool of untrained potential meant to the nation's commerce.

It was a broad and sweeping vision.

Governments could and should take a direct hand in reducing or eliminating unemployment through research, vocational guidance, work initiatives, active work with industry, public works projects and finally through an unemployment insurance scheme. Labour exchanges could also "work with the parents and teachers of young people about to leave school," he suggested, "and help them select occupations which they would enjoy, which are not in decline and for which they have the necessary aptitudes."

Stewart served as the first director of the Employment Service of Canada from 1918 until 1922. When the fledgling service was effectively halved by Mackenzie King's incoming Labour government, Stewart left his position. He moved to Chicago and began to work for the Rockefeller Foundation and for the Amalgamated Clothing Workers Union. He remained in the U.S. for eighteen years, earning a Ph.D. from Columbia in 1926.

In 1940, Mackenzie King summoned him back to Canada. The National Employment Service and Unemployment Insurance Commission was being established, and historian John Hunter believes the prime minister probably enticed Stewart back into Canada's public service by appealing to his sense of patriotic responsibility. Stewart served as Deputy Minister of Labour from 1940 until 1942, during the crucial era when the Employment Service Commission and the National Employment Service were established.

Processes became more mechanized. People were ever more closely supervised. Working conditions were as bad or worse than they had ever been. And resentment continued to grow.

Voices in the wilderness

The failure of the 1919 strike dashed the dreams of unskilled or low-skilled workers for a strong and unified voice. It would be thirty years before industrial unions would again gather enough strength to get employers and governments to pay attention to their needs.

On the prairies, the seeds of discontent fell on more fertile ground. Agricultural productivity had fuelled expansion before the war, but the prairie economy had begun to weaken. Wheat and wheat flour continued to be Canada's major export, but there was a glut on the market, and prices dropped sharply, just as farm operating costs increased, thanks in large part to tariffs.

Farmers were already deeply angry. Despite promises their sons would be exempt from conscription, the government had reneged and begun calling them up in the final year of the war. Now, as their pleas to government for tariff reductions went unanswered, Canadian farmers began to consider that the central government could not or would not address their needs. They decided to assert their position in the political arena and the United Farmers Party began to spring up throughout English Canada. In 1920, the National Progressive Party was established.

Labour began to grope its way into the political arena, as well. After the 1919 provincial election in Ontario, the United Farmers combined forces with a small labour party to form the government. And at the federal level, J. S. Woodsworth, social reformer and one of the men arrested in the Winnipeg strike, was elected in 1921, along with William Irvine of Calgary, on a labour platform.

Even within the two traditional parties the political winds were shifting. In the years immediately following the war, both the Conservatives and Liberals changed leaders. Wilfrid Laurier died in 1919, leaving the Liberals without a clear successor. They held their first leadership convention and found a new leader in William Lyon Mackenzie King. He was well educated, shrewd and ambitious and had been the country's first Labour minister.

Shortly afterward, exhausted and disheartened by the lack of appreciation for his achievements overseas, Robert Borden resigned. And the hard-working, inflexible and staunchly conservative Arthur Meighen took over the leadership of the Unionist Government.

An election followed in 1921. King's Liberals won although, for the first time, Canadians elected a minority parliament. Regional differences were clearly evident in the voting patterns. Canada's post-war electorate, under the strains of continuing immigration, urbanization, industrialization and the regional economic disparities, reflected the absence of any unifying direction to Canadian life, so central in the years before.

A consummate political player, King was also a former labour negotiator, chosen as Liberal leader partly on the basis of his apparent understanding of the problems inherent in the modern industrial workplace. In his dense and theoretical book, *Industry and Humanity*, King endorsed such revolutionary concepts as the eight-hour day and the forty-eight-hour week. The new prime minister's sentiments notwithstanding, it would be several decades before such notions found their way into legislation.

New tools and changing skills

The Great War had propelled Canada into a new technological era. And in the years that followed, the skills and abilities people needed to assure career and employment success began to change.

On the one hand, for the factory workers of the day, work was being deliberately "de-skilled." In search of ever greater efficiencies, manufacturers and industrial employers had developed complex interconnecting systems of machines and workers, all of which functioned under the close direction of a supervisor or manager. In workplaces such as these, Taylorism continued to define management techniques.

Trained craftspeople no longer plied a whole range of skills to create a finished product. Instead, with certain basic abilities and a little instruction, an unskilled person could be quickly trained to complete a single task, and then pass the product on down the line to the next worker, who would do the same.

Ironically, at the same time, the war had furthered the development of a wide range of highly specialized products, sophisticated machines that ran the gamut from cars to farm equipment to typewriters and adding machines. And for almost every innovation that appeared, whole new industries would follow.

Glimpses of the future, and the workplace of the future, were visible in 1919, when Alcock and Brown made the first flight across the Atlantic; in 1922, when Armand Bombardier invented the first practical snowmobile; and in 1923, when baby-faced Foster Hewitt delivered his first hockey broadcast on radio.

Slowly at first, but ever more insistently, the demand grew for a new type of worker, someone with business skills, supervisory skills, engineering expertise, or with the technical and mechanical skills to operate the new technology, as well as to service, maintain and repair it.

Upgrading workplace skills

The Technical Educational Act of 1919 signalled Ottawa's continued interest in developing the skills of Canadian workers. The act created a ten-year, multi-million dollar program of conditional grants to the provinces. The federal government promised to cover up to 50 percent of provincial expenditures for technical and vocational training. Provinces could use the money to build schools, pay staff and train teachers to do the work.

The potential for jurisdictional disputes was carefully contained from the outset. Late in 1920, in a speech at the first annual Conference on Technical Education, the Minister of Labour at the time, Senator

Gideon Robertson, made it very clear that the provinces had full authority over educational matters. He assured delegates that the federal government only wanted to help the provinces provide technical training in an efficient and standardized way. The federal role, he said, was gathering and dispensing information about the labour market as well as providing other printed materials.

Over the following decade, most of the provinces would respond with programs. Across the country, in various ways, technical and vocational schools and courses would be established, as nearly eight million dollars in federal funds flowed into provincial coffers.

Despite advances, however, the early 1920s would prove to be grim for most Canadian workers. Technical skills were of little use in the absence of jobs and, with the post-war collapse of international trade, unemployment was on the rise.

Through its Employment Service, the federal government was already involved in the employment needs of Canadian workers. The service was a network of provincial employment bureaus to which the federal government administered financial grants. There were about seventy employment bureaus in operation across the country and, before the decade was out, the Employment Service could boast some 1,900,000 male job placements. However, it says much about the effectiveness of the service and the volatility of the labour market, that many of the jobs were temporary and about a quarter of the people placed in those jobs held them for less than a week.

Initially farm interests in the west opposed the Employment Service. They wanted a pool of cheap labour and did not appreciate the government's efforts to find alternative work for the urban unemployed. Opposition faded, however, once the Employment Service began arranging for workers from B.C. and eastern Canada to work on prairie farms during harvest, a movement that continued until the 1950s.

> "New materials demand new methods and new methods fling challenges to old conventions."
>
> Lawren Harris, 1921

The not-so-roaring '20s

Seen from the perspective of the present day, the 1920s was a decade of flappers, Mary Pickford, Rudolph Valentino and unbridled growth and prosperity. It is arguable how accurate that image was even in the United States. Canada's experience of growth appeared to be more muted: the pockets of prosperity that did open up proved not to be big enough to meet the needs of all Canadians.

The U.S. was prospering, certainly, and investment dollars were rolling north, building factories to produce rubber, chemicals and clothing in industrial centres around the Great Lakes. Canada's north expanded, as well, as minerals from the Canadian Shield found markets in both this country and the U.S.

By the middle of the decade, the numbers of new immigrants began to rise again and, in western Canada, farming communities had resumed their growth. Although agriculture continued as its mainstay, the western economy diversified to some degree. Hydroelectric plants began to churn in Manitoba and British Columbia and the newly found reserves in Turner Valley sparked Alberta's oil and gas industry.

What was good for one region in this sprawling nation, however, wasn't necessarily good for another. Industry and influence were becoming increasingly concentrated in the central provinces and the drag was stronger than the Maritime economy could tolerate. The Maritime's wartime export market had disappeared on the heels of the armistice. Prices for coal and iron dropped and many of Cape Breton's miners were unemployed. The preferential freight rates, lost when the Maritimes' Intercolonial Railway had been integrated into CNR (Canadian National Railway), were not re-established.

Throughout much of the country, in fact even in its most prosperous regions, working people had to struggle to make ends meet. In 1929, the federal Department of Labour estimated that a Canadian family of four required an annual income of $1,200 to $1,500 a year just to supply the minimum comforts of life. With the '20s supposedly at full "roar," 60 percent of men and 82 percent of working women earned poverty wages of less than $1,000 a year.[3] The two-income household was a rarity so, in reality, half the working population of Canada was poor as the Roaring '20s ended. For these people, the need was basic survival: to put food on the table and hang onto the roof over their heads.

The City of Toronto Archives

1926: Thanksgiving Day, veterans march through the streets of Toronto protesting the lack of jobs.

As if that wasn't bad enough, the situation was about to get much worse. On October 29, 1929, the New York stock market crashed. Canada and the western world had become highly dependent upon U.S. currency and America's economic crisis soon reverberated around the globe. Many people thought the "correction" would be short-lived, but they were to be sorely disappointed. Demand dropped for Canadian lumber, fish, minerals, and pulp and paper. The price of wheat plummeted.

As the Dirty Thirties descended and the economy shrank, the scourge of unemployment was felt as never before. In 1929, Department of Labour figures estimated that approximately 3 percent of Canadian workers were unemployed and looking for work. Within a year, that number had almost quadrupled, to 11 percent, or over half a million people. By the time the Depression hit bottom, more than double that number, roughly 25 percent of the workforce, couldn't find work.

Both manufacturing and agriculture took the hit. About a third of the jobs in the manufacturing sector were lost. Net farm income fell from over $417 million in 1929 to $109 million in 1933.

Canadians lucky enough to hold down a job during these brutal years fared well enough, as wages remained constant for a time while prices fell. Eventually, however, even wages came down, as most government employees and many in large organizations took a wage cut of 15 percent or more. Some of the craft unions voted to work half time, sharing the other half of their work with other union members.

The arrival of the Dirty Thirties

As the Depression deepened, regional disparities became more evident. No part of the country escaped the economic upheaval, but few were as badly off as those on the Canadian prairies. What the failing economy didn't do to prairie farmers, Mother Nature did. Drought settled in as the decade began and, aside from occasional brief respites, it persisted until 1937. The fragile soils had been ploughed too deeply, the land dried out, the winds picked up and dust storms raged. During those few intervals when the wind dropped and some rain fell, grasshoppers descended. By 1937, two out of every three Canadians living in rural Saskatchewan needed assistance.

In those years, Canada had few social security measures, outside of a small old age pension of $20 a month for needy seniors. Some provinces had also legislated a Mother's Allowance, which directed a pittance to widows and deserted wives with two or more children.

Other relief or welfare programs did exist and, when the Depression was at its worst, no less than one in ten Canadian families relied on them. "Relief" in this guise was modeled on nineteenth century "poor-relief" systems. Despite the crushing weight of the country's economic problems, it was generally felt that the poor had no one to blame but themselves. Applying for welfare was a humiliating experience and relief benefits were available only after people had given up virtually all possessions of any value, including their clothes and pets.

1931: Mother Nature adds to the nation's grief as the soil dries out and dust storms blow away what had been rich, productive land.

In Nova Scotia and New Brunswick, most poor families were forced to take up residence in the county poorhouses. Relief programs put a tremendous financial burden on civic and provincial governments. In 1930, nationwide, roughly $18 million was spent on relief expenditures. Five years later, that outlay had ballooned to $173 million, so stretching the finances of some civic and provincial governments that they faced bankruptcy.

In 1930, the Tories took power in Ottawa, with their new leader R. B. Bennett promising to end unemployment or die in the attempt. He did neither but, as the crisis deepened, he did take some action, providing federal grants worth $20 million to the provinces to help them cover relief expenditures and implement public works programs to create jobs. His efforts barely made a dent in the problem.

Young single men were not eligible for relief outside of workhouses and many took to riding the rails across the country, looking for food or following rumours of work in other centres. In 1932, Bennett's government decided to take control of the problem and used the Department of National Defense to establish work camps, most of them in remote areas.

Run under strict military discipline, the camps put men to work clearing brush and building roads, for which they supposedly earned a dollar a day. Once their "expenses" had been deducted, however, the amount dropped to about twenty cents. Conditions in the camps were often shameful. The food was dreadful, accommodations were rudimentary and services like latrines were inadequate to the numbers of people in residence. Over the next four years, upwards of one hundred thousand young men were sent to live in these camps, which some referred to as slave camps.

By the middle of the decade, a deep discouragement and resentment had built up not only in the relief camps, but also among the million or more people unemployed across the country. It was a time of incredible poverty and destitution. Some families depended completely on bread lines and soup kitchens.

The National Archives of Canada

1930: R. B. Bennett won the election for the Tories promising to end unemployment. But by 1935, he had failed, and lost the election to Mackenzie King.

Communities respond once again

Immediately after the First World War, successful businessman Horace A. Moses founded an organization he called Junior Achievement to interest young people in starting up their own business. Moses saw entrepreneurship as a means for young people to learn the benefits of self-sufficiency. His school-based program was one of the first to understand the holistic nature of career development and hence emphasized both workforce readiness and life skills. Eight years after its inception, Junior Achievement involved young people in many countries, plus thousands of workplace-based mentors who continued to emphasize the principles Moses had laid out at the close of the First World War.

1935: The trek to Ottawa to meet with Prime Minister R. B. Bennett became known as The Depression Train.

Throughout the post-war period and the Depression, many community service agencies began advocating on behalf of the needy and the disadvantaged. In major urban centres, religious and charitable organizations expanded their missions to provide for transient or homeless men, including veterans. The scope of the demands, however, far exceeded their ability to meet them.

The Great Depression did see the formation of another raft of community agencies concerned with the welfare of Canadians. For instance, Goodwill Industries (1935) and the Woodgreen Community Centre (1937) formed in Toronto and, once again, the Vancouver YWCA found itself providing courses and placing women in jobs throughout the '30s.

And yet, in Canada, there were no professionals trained in the field of career guidance and counselling at the time. And the counselling available from charitable and religious organizations tended to focus on basic survival needs like food and shelter. When assistance of this kind did address working needs, it tended to focus on finding work, any kind of work. Long term vocational goals and a plan to achieve them were generally not a part of the working person's life. During this time, public policy and opinion converged on one issue and one issue alone: jobs.

"When the Depression came, our world stopped, and we got off."

James H. Gray, 1929

As much as the Great War before it, the Great Depression had a deep and lasting impact on Canadian society. As it demonstrated the vagaries of 20th century life, it forged a new political and social awareness. And it amplified the workers' needs for help and direction. In the shattered dreams of people who had once prided themselves on their self-sufficiency and the disappointment of those who had fought valiantly for their country and returned to an indifferent government, there was a dawning realization that Canada's political and social systems were inadequate. And out of this recognition, the political capital of individual Canadians grew.

Recognition of another kind of bridge financing: Between jobs

New political parties were created to offer Canadians choices. From the west came the Cooperative Commonwealth Confederation (CCF) and the Social Credit, both with well-defined social agendas. In Quebec, the Union Nationale emerged to tackle traditional parties and their positions on economics, as well as Quebec's unique cause, cultural preservation.

Pushed by a growing pressure from the left, mainstream government began to provide assistance to people in need. Probably the most important new social program came from Ottawa. Bennett had tabled the Unemployment Insurance bill as part of his 1935 New Deal; however, an election later that year overturned Bennett's Tories and gave the country back to Mackenzie King who referred the UI bill to the judicial committee of the Privy Council of the United Kingdom, then Canada's final court of appeal.

> "You referred to us as not wanting work. Give any of us work and see whether we will work."
>
> Arthur (Slim) Evans, 1935 labour organizer who led a delegation of striking relief camp workers to Ottawa.

In 1937, the Privy Council ruled that Bennett's bill was unconstitutional because it invaded provincial jurisdiction without the explicit approval of the provinces, and several provinces opposed federal legislation on Unemployment Insurance. Once again, the jurisdictional split between the central government and the provinces stood in the way of decisive action.

Unemployment remained high and government began to direct some of its attention to the worrisome numbers of idle young people who had begun to appear on the streets. The Unemployment and Agricultural Assistance Act of 1937 was its response. While providing funds for the vocational training of jobless men and women between eighteen and thirty who were registered with the National Employment Service, the act also stressed the need for adequate counselling, guidance and placement services.

In 1940, King tabled his own Unemployment Insurance bill. The consultation with the provinces was more agreeable in the context of the war effort. And the Unemployment Insurance Act finally became the law of the land, establishing both a compulsory contributory insurance scheme and a revamped Employment Service with a truly national mandate.

Spending for jobs

Taken together, the Unemployment and Agricultural Assistance Act and the Unemployment Insurance bill were nowhere near sufficient to respond to the swollen need the nation now confronted. But at least some of the people in power were considering constructive ways to respond. And not a moment too soon.

In the latter half of the '30s, as the national economy shunted slowly toward recovery, it became obvious that average working people were not among those on the gravy train. To some extent, the economy was on the mend, but although the business climate had clearly improved, incomes continued to sag and unemployment remained high.

Hamstrung by the constitutional limitations on their powers and reticent to challenge traditional methods of economic management, both federal and provincial governments seemed stymied by the situation. In 1938, the economy began to slump again and Ottawa policy chiefs began to talk cautiously of a "stimulative deficit."[4] If people and businesses weren't ready to spend the economy back to health, they argued, Ottawa would have to do it for them.

Glenbow Archives

1933: Heroes and Bums. Protest scenes like this continued the cry for help from men who felt their war efforts had been largely ignored by an indifferent government.

In relatively short order, the government began to fund a variety of work projects and subsidized numerous housing and construction projects. The youth training program alone would receive nearly $3.5 million over the next five years.[5]

The staunchly anti-interventionist government had undergone a conversion, at least rhetorically. "The old days of laissez-faire, and the-devil-take-the-hindmost have gone for good,"[6] proclaimed the Liberal Finance Minister Charles Dunning in 1939, suggesting that the federal government had recognized that government intervention was necessary to improve the economy and create jobs.

Within months, the spectre of war was upon the nation again and many of the decisions politicians had been afraid to make were made for them. In the end, it was government spending on yet another war effort that finally put Canadians back to work.

[1] Desmond Morton, *A Short History of Canada* (Toronto: McClelland & Stewart, 1992).
[2] Ibid.
[3] Ibid.
[4] Ibid.
[5] "A Review of Federal Legislation Relating to Technical and Vocational Education in Canada" – Donald Glendenning, Programs Branch, Dept. of Manpower and Immigration.
[6] Craig Brown, editor, *History of Canada* (Toronto: Key Porter, 2000).

POST-WAR Prosperity AND A Replenished Labour Supply

CHAPTER 4

16,000 aircraft
741 naval vessels
3,302 landing craft
410 cargo vessels
800,000 transport vehicles
50,000 tanks
148,000 heavy guns
2 million tons of chemicals and explosives
133 million rounds of heavy ammunition
5 billion rounds of small arms' ammunition

1943: Historic Quebec meeting of wartime leaders: Prime Minister William Lyon Mackenzie King, U.S. President Theodore Roosevelt and British Prime Minister Winston Churchill.

The National Archives of Canada

It was quite a shopping list. Especially given that everything on it was Made in Canada. As he solemnly intoned his country's declaration of war against Germany in 1939, Liberal Prime Minister Mackenzie King was still casting about for ways to revitalize the nation and avoid the mistakes of the First World War. On all accounts, despite his initial reluctance to enter the fray, King would enjoy remarkable success.

Barely eighteen months later, with Canadian troops on guard in Britain and Royal Canadian Navy corvettes providing protection for British convoys in the western Atlantic, Canada's national economy was booming. Sixteen munitions factories across the country produced a range of materials for the war, including military vehicles, mine sweepers, smaller coastal vessels and escort vessels like the corvettes.

Gone just as suddenly were the high levels of unemployment that had so troubled the Canadian economy in the 1930s. More than half a million Canadian workers who had been unemployed prior to the war were quickly absorbed, either into the armed forces or the rapidly expanding workforce. Even these numbers, however, were not sufficient to meet the growing demand and young people, women and seniors were mobilized as well. By 1943, 1.2 million Canadians had found work in war industries, many in factories that hadn't even existed as the war began.

Most of the new materials were manufactured by private sector companies that had quickly retooled to make products unlike anything previously seen on their assembly lines. The John Inglis Company switched from washing machines to gun components. General Motors in Regina retooled to turn out naval guns. The Canadian Car and Foundry in Fort William (now part of Thunder Bay) produced dive bombers. And from the National Steel Car Corporation at Malton, Ontario came the legendary Lancaster bombers.

The architect of the transformation in Canada's manufacturing sector was businessman and engineer C.D. Howe, the government's Minister of Munitions and Supply, who later became known as "minister of everything." During the war, Howe's department handed out government contracts worth billions of dollars, dramatically expanding Canada's industrial and manufacturing infrastructure. In British Columbia, a ship building industry grew. In eastern Canada, steel production doubled. Aluminum smelters were built. Entirely new industries like nuclear power and petrochemicals came into being.

As Denmark, Norway, Belgium, the Netherlands and even France succumbed to Hitler's advance, Canada's military forces and materials were ever more in demand. By late 1942, there were five Canadian divisions overseas. Canadian infantrymen took part in the advance up the mainland of Italy and stormed the Normandy beaches when the Allies landed in 1944 to begin the liberation of Europe.

Ultimately, over a million of this country's men and women served in the Second World War, often on the frontlines, with great strength and courage.

The costs of war

Just as it had a quarter of a century earlier, however, the war effort came at a heavy price. By the time the fighting was over, total Canadian casualties numbered about forty-two thousand. Although significantly lower than the First World War, the numbers included, once again, many of the country's youngest and most promising people.

In financial terms, as well, the costs were high. In all, Ottawa spent more than four billion dollars on the war and Canada's national debt quadrupled.

These were pivotal years for Canada and the federal government's actions were absolutely critical to the success both of the war effort and the adjustment period that followed. As early as 1943, prodded by memories of the unrest following the First World War and by the growing

National Archives of Canada

1942:
C. D. Howe, Minister of Munitions and Supply, visits a war products factory.

1941:
Bren Gun Girl. Young women and many seniors were mobilized as the demand for workers increased.

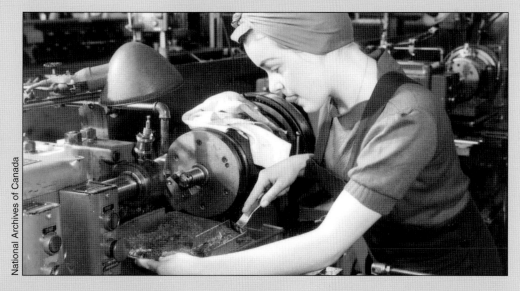

National Archives of Canada

1941:
Lunch-time break. By 1943, more than a million Canadians were working in the war industry.

National Archives of Canada

influence of the CCF with its strong social agenda, King's government had begun to focus on policies to help the country prepare for peace.

Money for peace

As much as their political leaders, Canadians had feared the end of the war, concerned that it could herald a return to the unemployment and hopelessness of the Depression. Now, having seen the impact the federal government could have when it applied itself fully to a problem, they demanded the same sort of leadership in managing the post-war economy. "The propaganda of the thirties had always been that the government had no money, couldn't do anything about it and that's the way things were," said Joseph Levitt, a returning soldier who later became a history professor. "But the war taught people a lot. It was a matter of common sense and simple to understand that if the government could find money for war, they could find it for peace."

Fortuitously, many of the preconditions for greater government involvement were now in place. Taxation levels had increased dramatically and the federal civil service had more than doubled in size over the course of the war. The huge wartime debt caused few public officials to panic. British economist John Maynard Keynes's theory that government debt encouraged economic growth had become popular during the war. At the same time, the foundations of a New Social Order, as King called it, had been established.

Unemployment Insurance had come into effect in 1941 and, in 1945, the first Baby Bonus cheques began to arrive in Canadian mailboxes, providing family allowances of up to eight dollars a month for every child under the age of sixteen. There were old age pensions as well as provincial assistance programs for abandoned mothers and for the blind, though these pre-war programs continued to be funded parsimoniously.

Programs for returning veterans were administered by the newly established Department of Veterans' Affairs. About 200,000 veterans went back to work with their previous employers, thanks to the dictates of the Reinstatement Act. Another 150,000 used veterans' educational grants to attend university or college. Still others went into farming or fishing using grants offered by the Veterans' Land Act.

The National Housing Act was legislated to guarantee low cost mortgages. An Industrial Development Board began to plan for the retooling needs of Canadian businesses. In all, the government set aside an astonishing amount, some $3.12 billion, to fund the transitional agenda.

Probably the single most important factor affecting the government's ability to manage the transition more effectively this time around was the country's enormously expanded industrial base. Under the guiding hand of C. D. Howe and his team of seconded businessmen, some of them working for token payment of a dollar a year, Canada had emerged from the Second World War as the world's fifth largest industrial power, with dramatically increased export potential.

Success breeds success, particularly in the high wire arenas of political power, and it was only logical that the newly created Ministry of Reconstruction should go to the man who had demonstrated such zeal

1940: Co-operative Commonwealth Federation (CCF) leaders, including a young Tommy Douglas (far left), were a growing political force.

as Minister of Munitions and Supply, none other than C. D. Howe. Tax incentives and write-offs had been the principal tactics used by Howe to convince Canadian industrialists to retool for war production and now he plied the same tools to persuade them to convert to peace-time activities.

Most of the twenty-eight crown corporations Howe's war-time ministry had established were shut down or sold, although he did find ways to protect and extend the activities of two which had added totally new industries to Canada's business landscape: Polysar (petrochemicals) and Eldorado Nuclear (atomic energy). Trans Canada Airlines, established just before the war, also remained under government control.

What was good for business, this time around, was also good for workers. Following a brief slowdown in 1945-46, the nation's industrial output rapidly grew beyond its wartime peak. In factories, plants and foundries, industrial technology had become more advanced, changing the way hundreds of thousands of people worked. It had also created new jobs. The total number of jobs in the manufacturing sector had doubled during the war years, providing employment for some 1,240,000 people by 1946. And most of the 250,000 women who had worked during the war either returned home to their more traditional roles or moved back into the lower-paying jobs they had held before the conflict. At the same time, industrial wages increased, from about $20 a week to over $30. Unemployment held steady at around 3 percent.

Beyond North America, the rest of the industrialized world was in a shambles. As devastated European countries took advantage of the generous financial aid program known as the Marshall Plan offered by the U.S. government, Canadian business also reaped the rewards. In relatively short order, traditional export markets were re-established, and international trade in Canadian goods and products expanded even further, enhancing the country's position among twenty-three founding nations as the historic General Agreement on Tariffs and Trade was signed in 1947.

State of organized labour

Even Canada's labour movement had been strengthened by the war; wartime shifts in worker supply and demand having bestowed new clout and confidence. However improved the employment climate during the war years, it had not been free of labour confrontations. Companies that refused to accept unions frequently found themselves dealing with slowdowns and strikes. In 1943 alone, some 400 strikes took more than 200,000 workers off the job for periods of time.

As for productivity, there is no question that labour unrest took its toll. In the automobile industry, in textiles, rubber, steel, forestry, electrical manufacturing and mining about 240,000 striking workers were off the job for a total of nearly seven million workdays in 1946 and '47 alone. Tangible gains for labour were made as a result of these actions and it was becoming increasingly clear that industrial workers were no longer prepared to play the role of silent cogs in management's wheels.

By the time it had ended, the Second World War had transformed Canadian society. Individual Canadians saw the world differently. Canada's business community had been completely rebuilt. Workers had demanded and been awarded greater respect. And, in some quarters at least, vocational and career counselling had even become a valued service.

Statistics, psychometrics and "satisfying careers"

The Second World War not only transformed industry and Canadian society at large. It was a pivotal time in the growth of career and vocational counselling, as the field of psychology, a phenomenon of the 20th century, began to emphasize "applied psychology" as counselling was then known. As discussed in Chapter 2, vocational guidance had received some attention prior to the First World War when a Royal Commission was formed, but the wars and economic depression intervened.

"Fitting the man to the job" was a priority for the military. From the first hours of the war until its final days, the effective placement of recruits ranked as a primary concern and classification of personnel was one of many areas in which the still emerging discipline of psychology was found to be of value. Although a new practice in the Canadian military, psychological assessment to assist in the selection and placement of veterans had been in place in the United States during the First World War.

In 1938, with rumours of war growing louder by the day, professors of psychology from various Canadian universities had banded together to form the Canadian Psychological Association (CPA). Their primary objective was to assure that psychological techniques and expertise were used appropriately and effectively during the coming war.

A number of psychologists, all members of this new association, were hired by the RCAF. E. A. Bott, S. N. F. Chant, C. R. Myers, E. I. Signori and D. C. Williams worked together between 1939 and 1941 to develop a variety of assessment techniques and psychometric tests to be used in the selection and training of aircrews for the British Commonwealth Air Training Plan (BCATP).

Late in 1941, when Bott and Myers relocated to England to team up with the RAF, Chant and the others remained to carry out the work required in Canada. A year later, Chant established a directorate of Personnel Selection and Research.

Once the war had ended, the government shifted its attention to the re-establishment needs of veterans and Chant was named Director-General of the Rehabilitation Department of Veterans' Affairs. Many of the tests and assessments he and his colleagues had developed during the war were now adapted to help the armed forces re-integrate military personnel into civilian life.

Most veterans returned home from the Second World War to a hero's welcome. After they had marched in the parades, attended the parties and received the accolades from the Welcome Home Citizens' Committees, finding their way back into civilian life meant finding their way into the right line of work. And the federal government had allocated about $750 million to help them do just that. Ian Mackenzie, the Minister of Veterans' Affairs in 1945, put it this way: "Canada's rehabilitation belief is that the answer to civil re-establishment is a job and the answer to a job is fitness and training for that job. Our ambition is that the men and women who have taken up arms in the defense of their country and their ideals of freedom shall not be penalized for the time they have spent in the services. And our desire is that they shall be fitted in every way possible to take their place in Canada's civil and economic life."

Resuming a life as civilians

Gone were the days when strong arms and a broad back were the primary criteria for work, and "fit" was simply a matter of matching the body to the task. The workplace had changed dramatically in the course of the war and each of the returning veterans had changed as well. Years abroad had given many Canadians their first glimpse of the world beyond their own communities. Most returned with significantly altered perspectives on life and very different goals and aspirations. Many had acquired new skills but they also brought home the internal scars of war; making the transition to civilian life wasn't easy for many.

But for anyone looking for a way back into civilian life, decisions about work and careers and how and where to apply those skills had become overriding concerns. There was a growing recognition that, for many people, some form of vocational or occupational counselling would be critical to their ability to make a successful transition. Canadian industry, for example, had shown considerable interest in the military counselling processes and had even provided information to support their application in the post-war workplace.

Given the enormous numbers the re-establishment programs had to deal with, the procedures were remarkably effective. Before being discharged, military personnel met with what Veterans' Affairs called "occupational counsellors" who were charged with administering aptitude and intelligence tests and providing information regarding the various government-sponsored employment programs, educational opportunities, land grants and home-building schemes.

RCAF veterans were assisted in their transition by being given a "personnel assessment" which was "essentially, a scientific method of assessment with, as the end result, the discovery of each person's most satisfying type of career," observed E. N. Stanford, writing in the December 1944 issue of *Canadian Business*. "Businessmen have helped the RCAF research, compile employment statistics, build up job analyses and prognosticate (as far as anyone dares) the relative opportunities in each kind of job in terms of pay, promotion, competition and so on."

About one hundred people from within the armed forces had been trained to work as RCAF "personnel counsellors," according to Stanford. These were the people stationed at RCAF bases and in regional demobilization centres who actually did the assessments, provided the necessary information and helped each individual explore the range of options open to them.

Outside of the armed forces, in the offices, plant floors and hiring halls of the expanding industrial workplace, the need for informed counsel regarding work and careers had increased as well, although the government of the day was less inclined to see itself as the appropriate agency to meet it. In the years following the war, therefore, the vocational and career counselling needs of these people tended to fall, as they had for decades, to the agencies that made up the not-for-profit sector.

In 1947, the Soeurs de Notre Dame du Bon Conseil initiated the Centre Social d'Immigracion to assist Second World War veterans and immigrants to Canada who were fleeing the economic devastation in which much of the world had been left after the war. Not-for-profit organizations across the country helped ease the transition of returning servicemen and, to a lesser degree, women back into Canadian worklife.

Vocational guidance and the introduction of applied psychology

The war had still been in progress when Dr. Clarence Hincks, a professional from another related field, mental health, took his personal crusade for better treatment of people with psychological problems to the YMCA. Too many young men were ending up in mental institutions, said the general director of the National Committee for Mental Hygiene, "because they had no where else to go."

What these individuals really needed, Hincks believed, was vocational guidance to help them get a start in life. Once the war was over, he added, demobilized forces personnel would be returning home in need of similar assistance.

Hincks' plea struck a chord with the YMCA in Toronto, which had already identified the employment needs of young men as a problem area and had been considering ways to become more directly involved. During the war, with many married women working, there was a widespread belief that juvenile delinquency was on the rise. While the statistical evidence suggests otherwise, the belief that young males growing up with fewer parental controls required the aid of social agencies became quite entrenched. In 1943, the Toronto YMCA established its Counselling Service for young men and youths.

"Applied psychology" was not an established course of study in Canadian universities at the time. For Gerald P. Cosgrave, however, a professor in the University of Toronto's psychology department, it was a subject of abiding interest and passion.

Cosgrave, too, was a member of the new Canadian Psychological Association (CPA) and, on the Committee on Aviation, had contributed significantly to the development of tests used to assess aircrews. A quiet, unassuming loner with a postgraduate degree in philosophy, Cosgrave had opted to leave the CPA project in 1941. Conscientious, highly meticulous and fussy, he simply was not cut out

for experimental work, according to some of his colleagues. Shortly thereafter, however, when the YMCA offered him a position as the director of its new Counselling Service, it was precisely the sort of challenge in applied psychology Gerald Cosgrave had been looking for.

Cosgrave's approach to vocational counselling began with a one-on-one interview. The process evolved over a series of sessions, which included testing and assessment. All test results were interpreted by a counsellor and subsequently reviewed by Dr. Cosgrave, then presented to the individual in a personal interview and a written report.

Gerald Cosgrave

Frank G. Lawson

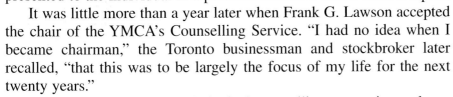

It was little more than a year later when Frank G. Lawson accepted the chair of the YMCA's Counselling Service. "I had no idea when I became chairman," the Toronto businessman and stockbroker later recalled, "that this was to be largely the focus of my life for the next twenty years."

Cosgrave's view that psychological counselling was an integral part of vocational guidance found a happy match in Frank Lawson. Lawson was convinced that young people needed guidance in three different aspects of their lives. First, he felt they needed what people in the vocational guidance movement advocated—to discover the kind of work they were able to do and would enjoy. Second, many also required education or training to strengthen their abilities. Finally, he said, young people often needed help in dealing with negative attitudes that might otherwise hold them back.

Working with Cosgrave, Lawson quickly became a fervent supporter of the counselling process. Before they were finished, the two would spend all of twenty years together at the helm of the Toronto YMCA Counselling Service, forging a partnership that would contribute significantly to the development of career counselling theory and programs in Canada.

At its best, the vocational or occupational counselling available to people in the post-war years was supervised by trained psychologists, as it was in the Toronto YMCA's Counselling Service and the Jewish Vocational Service. Sophisticated vocational counselling services such as these were rare in Canada, however.

Thanks to the booming economy at the time, unemployment was low and the need for guidance and direction on the part of average workers was perhaps not as apparent as it had been just a few years earlier. It still existed nonetheless and, aside from the efforts of agencies such as the YMCA, YWCA and the Jewish Vocational Service in major cities as well as Montreal's Soeurs de Notre Dame, the need was largely unmet.

Out of the forces and back to school

If the wave of change set in motion by the war and its aftermath had a transforming effect on government, business and workers, its impact was even more pronounced on institutions of higher learning. In three short years, between 1944 and 1947, Canadian university enrollment doubled, as 150,000 veterans poured out of the military and onto campuses throughout the nation. The post-secondary educational system had never seen anything like it and, by the time the wave had passed, it would never be the same again.

Believing that Canada's universities represented the best way to offer educational services to veterans, Ottawa provided funds for programs aimed at the needs of the returning forces personnel. Across the country, Canadian universities expanded to meet the growing demand, adding staff and faculty and, in some cases, new facilities.

"Every college from coast to coast is bulging like a football stadium on a fine October Saturday afternoon," was how Gerald Anglin described it in *Maclean's* magazine on March 1, 1946. "Because [the University of Toronto] is Canada's largest university—almost double the size of any other, with 5,000 ex-servicemen boosting enrollment from 7,000 to 13,000 in the past year—Toronto's problem is the biggest."

In fact it was even more than Toronto could handle, as the downtown campus was simply too small. A satellite campus was established in nearby Ajax in a converted munitions plant, one of the many new factories that had sprung up in the area during the war.

Montreal's venerable McGill University mushroomed in a similar way, its total enrollment growing from 3,700 to 6,300. It too set up a branch operation, named Dawson College, twenty miles outside the city. Overcrowding was experienced on Canada's west coast as well, at the University of British Columbia, where some of the 7,000 students were required to attend classes in army huts that had been erected on campus grounds.

But classrooms in which to accommodate the swollen numbers were only part of the dilemma that confronted universities in these years. Institutional procedures and instructional techniques were affected as

well, as administrators and faculty were confronted for the first time with a very different breed of student—adults.

"As teachers we had a new type of challenge," said one professor at the University of Toronto. "A student with a realistic background which we respected, and with a purpose that was his own, as well as society's; one that had a little more urgency in it, in terms of time, than that to which we were accustomed."

The "Veteran at Varsity experience," as he called it, was "thrilling" for the academic community. But there were significant new stresses, as well. "We were conscious of queues for library books; of inadequate time, on our part, for research and on his part, inadequate research settings. Books often had to serve where original articles would have been better. Discussions gave way to lectures. The professor often had to adjust to a public-address system for the first time."

Despite such blocks and bottlenecks, teachers had done everything in their power to ensure that the needs of each individual were met. "If he didn't make good," said the professor, "he lost his Department of Veterans' Affairs support and that was disconcerting to all of us."

In order to ensure that veterans returned to employment as quickly and effectively as possible, the federal government established "placement services" on some university campuses. While the universities provided the specifics of education, the overriding concern in these government offices was to match workers (supply) to current and forecast jobs (demand), reflecting the same manpower planning policies that had been in place a quarter of a century earlier.

The Department of Veterans' Affairs also insisted that universities

1947: Montreal's McGill University saw its classrooms swell with war veterans eager to learn new skills that could lead to employment and better futures.

establish advisory services and appoint staff counsellors to inform veterans about their entitlements and provide counselling—especially regarding their work and careers. While some services were provided through such facilities during those years, few people were skilled in this specialized area and little vocational counselling was actually offered.

Occasionally, there were alternatives. The country's largest university, the University of Toronto, first set up a University Advisory Bureau and then, in 1948, a Placement Service of its own. "A group of colleges in the eastern United States had functions like this before we did," according to the Service's first director, Colonel J. K. Bradford. "And the purpose was the same. So I contacted them and we set up the centre in a similar way."

An engineer with a background in business and a returned veteran himself, Bradford was well positioned to head it up. "When industry heard about it they were very supportive," he recalled. So supportive, in fact, that in the Placement Service's first year of operation, forty-four companies visited the campus and conducted over three thousand interviews.

As in the government offices, job placement was the primary concern of the staff at the U of T centre, although some counselling was available for students struggling with adjustment problems and educational anxieties. Whenever a student's problems appeared to involve "real mental health matters," however, he or she was referred to the University Health Service.

Colonel Bradford recalls meeting with over ten thousand students in the nineteen years that he was Director of the Placement Service at U of T. His recollections of the meetings he had with students during those years provide a snapshot of the sort of lay counselling that professionals like Bradford offered people in need of vocational guidance.

"I found that all men had different personalities," he says. "And what was one man's choice wasn't another's. I wasn't a psychologist so I couldn't tell people what to do. I intentionally did not counsel them. It was my job to chat with people. I sat and listened. And they asked all the questions.

"I just helped them start. They did the work themselves. But I was speaking to people in industry all the time, so I knew where the jobs were. Today it's quite different. It's broken down into career planning and job listing and placement. But at the time we just talked with people and helped in any way we could."

Industrial growth and the welfare state

In such a manner, the fundamentals of career counselling were being conceived and born, even as the currents of economic change picked up all those people—veterans, graduates, counsellors, educators, businessmen, workers and politicians alike—and swept them into the longest sustained economic expansion the country had ever known.

Within a matter of ten years, five of them at war, the hardships of the previous two decades were largely erased. The western industrialized world was triumphant again and Canada had claimed her place in it.

Industry was now decisively in the driver's seat and the country was enjoying the ride. The economy expanded steadily as new industries sprouted and traditional industries powered up and grew. Jobs were abundant, more were being created.

Canada had become a "middle power," with a presence in NATO and a seat in the United Nations. It was a respected, confident nation. Manufacturing was the new powerhouse—manufacturing products on the retooled assembly lines that had themselves been retooled for war.

Canadians began their love affair with the automobile, as thousands upon thousands of Fords, Chryslers and Chevrolets rolled off the assembly lines in Oakville, Windsor and Oshawa.

Propelled by the new petrochemical industry, manufacturing entered the age of plastics and new products popped up on department-store shelves. The world of fashion got polyester and other synthetic fabrics. Housewives got clear plastic wrap for their leftovers.

These were the first years of the media explosion, with television sets placed in living rooms and small radios crackling on kitchen shelves. A steady stream of news, information and popular shows began to pour into Canadian households, much of it originating in the United States.

Highways were constructed, with major cities often at the hub of a network of roads. The Trans Canada Highway was completed in 1949. In Toronto, in 1954, the country's first subway went into service, at a cost of $54 million. Trans Canada Airlines was transformed from a military company to a company offering commercial flights. And everywhere industry sprouted, jobs were created.

Pent-up demand for homes converged with the long-term, low-cost mortgages offered under the National Housing Act to spark a construction boom and the country's major cities experienced a new surge of growth.

The federal government took more steps toward making Canada a "welfare state" removing the means test from old age pensions in 1951 and introducing a system of universal health care in 1958. The federal cost sharing and supplemental assistance program was introduced in 1956. Nova Scotia and New Brunswick at last agreed to phase out poorhouses and allow the destitute to receive benefits in their communities.

The consumer credit age began in 1951 as Diner's Club issued North America's first multi-use credit cards, outside of those issued by specific department stores. And there was plenty to buy: electric appliances like toasters and frying pans; Polaroid cameras to capture family birthdays; and drop-down record players to spin the hits of recording artists. From the pharmaceutical companies came antihistamines to combat allergy problems and penicillin to fight infections.

A new addition

The fourth decade drew to a close with the historic addition of Newfoundland and Labrador as Canada's newest province. After much debate and skepticism, a slim margin of votes brought the residents of this island in the mid-Atlantic into the Canadian fold. With its rich and colourful history, this new addition also brought to the Canadian table tremendous natural resources including fish and oil reserves.

Much of Canada's new prosperity was purchased with U.S. capital. American investment flooded north into Ontario's industrial heartland, then further north, into Quebec and Labrador, in quest of iron ore. American money helped finance the building of the St. Lawrence Seaway, Quebec's hydroelectric industry and railways into northern mining communities. It found its way, as well, to Alberta, where the 1947 oil discovery in Leduc began an oil and gas boom that would eventually make that province one of Canada's wealthiest.

POST-WAR
Adjusting
TO AN
Industrialized
Economy
AND THE EVOLUTION OF
VOCATIONAL GUIDANCE

I t was in the country's expanding urban centres, for the most part, that the growing prosperity of the post-war years made itself felt. With life in agricultural areas and coastal fishing villages becoming less viable, people continued to migrate to the cities. As the war ended, close to one in four Canadians still lived on farms. Over the next twenty-five years, their numbers would drop to one in fifteen. In the Atlantic fishery, in the '50s alone, the total working population would decline by 40 percent.

Despite such regional contractions, Canada's population continued to grow quickly. In 1946, the total was approximately twelve million. Fifteen years later, it had grown to over eighteen million. More than four million babies were born during these years and an additional two million new immigrants arrived, the vast majority of them from Europe. So powerful was the industrial job-creating machine, however, that unemployment remained relatively low. In 1956, a typical year, only 3.2 percent of the working population was unemployed.

In most large factories, low-skilled assembly line jobs were still the order of the day. But the increasing complexity of the workplace resulted in a growing demand for more "responsible"

National Archive of Canada

workers with "clear thinking skills" who could be promoted to positions as supervisors, administrators and managers. Attitudes in corporate circles had begun to change and, in a few cases at least, the top-down view of workers as "units of production" was slowly being redefined.[1]

Early in the 1950s, a handful of major companies like Westinghouse, Northern Electric and Canadian General Electric (CGE) began to take some responsibility for the career path of their workers. CGE, for example, introduced a "personnel assessment program" for employees. A major reorganization had taken place at CGE and this, it was felt, would help settle the corporate waters.

The program was designed by Dr. Herbert Moore, a Toronto industrial psychologist with the consulting firm Stevenson and Kellogg, and Olav Sorenson, a counsellor who had worked with Dr. Gerald Cosgrave at the Toronto YMCA's Counselling Service.

It was Sorenson who decided that the combination of psychological testing and feedback interviews as practiced by the Y's Counselling Service would be valuable to CGE employees as well. Following a day-long battery of tests, there was a "feedback interview" of approximately 1.5 hours. Career assessment of this kind was open to all employees, at their request, and some three thousand CGE staffers took advantage of it during the four years that it was in operation

These early glimmers of a new awareness of workplace needs were little more than that, however. For the most part, people were still on their own when it came to finding their way around in the world of work and nowhere was this more significant than among young people about to leave school.

> "In 1945, when the war ended, the men and women of the services came back, and the need for counselling was tremendous. Because when you take men and women away from their homes and ship them to a foreign country to fight a foreign war, when they come back they need to be integrated into our society…. They need job counselling. But not only them, their wives and children need help… because the man that went away is not the man who came back. And the wife that they left is not the wife that they came back to. And their children have grown beyond all recognition. So there is a great need for counselling."
>
> Frank Lawson

The birth of guidance

A new wave had begun to roll, a wave of "baby boomers" (those born after the war) whose needs, desires and appetites would reshape the country's workplace, economy and, ultimately, Canadian society itself. Education remained a world unto itself, however, and there were growing concerns for the future well-being of Canada's youth. In home-and-school association meetings, surveys, news articles and Royal Commission reports, the voices of both parents and employers could be heard calling for improvements in the way young people were taught.

Nationwide enrollment was climbing precipitously as half a million young Canadians reached school age every year. In classrooms throughout the country, however, traditional educational practices continued to hold sway. New buildings were built, additional teachers hired and spending on education spiralled. Teachers' wages tripled as their status in the community grew. School operating costs increased sevenfold and capital spending rose tenfold. But there was little information or counsel available to students trying to plan their working lives.

To businessmen, it was not just a case of workplace skills. Young people represented the future of the marketplace, as well, the nation's "human capital."

"By developing our educational system, expanding it and making it stronger, we will be cultivating the greatest of our natural resources, the people of Canada." So said Hugh Crombie, Chairman of the Canadian Manufacturers' Association's Education Committee. "Education increases income, purchasing power and productivity," he told the Maritime Branch of the National Vocational Guidance Association in 1949. Better education meant bigger pay cheques, and bigger pay cheques meant more active consumers.

"The more high school and college graduates there are in this country, the higher the standard of living we all will enjoy...the more prosperous customers business and industry will have."

Education, it seemed, was the new hope of the nation. The federal government, however gingerly, wanted to make its presence felt in education, a sector that the constitution reserved for the provinces. Despite opposition from Quebec, it made grants and funding available to universities. Using "equalization grants," it redistributed funds from wealthy provinces to have-not provinces, helping the governments of the latter afford educational and health care programs and social services more closely matched to those offered by the former.

To some, the lack of career or vocational guidance for Canadian students had been evident for years. As early as 1940, in fact, it had spurred a few visionary people to action. Morgan Parmenter was one. As a guidance teacher at Toronto's Danforth Technical School, he had become increasingly frustrated with the lack of materials available to help students understand the workplace into which they would soon take their first steps. In an attempt to respond to the need in his school, Parmenter had begun writing and mimeographing brief overviews—he called them occupational monographs—of some of the jobs that were open to students in the 1940s workplace.

As Dr. Clarence Hincks was advancing his concept of vocational guidance for young men to the YMCA, he was also lobbying for improvements in high school guidance for young people still in the school system. On discovering what Parmenter had been doing, Hincks encouraged him to continue his work and even helped him to create a small organization, the Vocational Guidance Centre, through which to distribute his monographs to other teachers.

In 1943, Parmenter was appointed Associate Professor of Guidance at the Ontario College of Education and his Vocational Guidance Centre was taken in along with him. A year later, in 1944, the Ontario Department of Education appointed a Director of Guidance and permitted different school boards to appoint guidance officers in secondary schools. And in the years following the war, similar developments occurred in other parts of the country.

Much of the so-called "guidance" of that era was based on IQ tests, which were used to assess a student's overall intelligence level. Developed early in the century, these tests were ultimately discredited, having been seen to reflect cultural and social biases. In the immediate post-war period, however, IQ test results were still used to direct students into different courses of study. Students with lower scores were generally channeled into vocational and technical programs, which did not have the same social status as academic programs.

Vocational guidance available to students in these technical and

Morgan Parmenter, author of *Success in the World of Work, You and Your Future and Exploring Occupations and Growing Up.*

vocational schools initially tended to focus on the occupations in high demand in the world of work. The quality and quantity of guidance varied considerably however, depending on the school district, the school and, ultimately, the teacher. At its best, when provided by teachers like Morgan Parmenter, vocational guidance included placement assistance, preceded by discussions about high demand occupations, often based on information provided by the skill/craft unions.

Educational guidance, as offered in academic high schools and collegiates, differed considerably. Academic planning for post-secondary education and a student's personal problems or family matters tended to be the primary concerns of educational guidance. In some schools, homeroom teachers were given guidance responsibilities along with their other duties. In other larger schools, guidance committees were set up to bring several teachers together to discuss a student's guidance needs.

At some point in their senior years, academic students would meet with the teacher assigned to be their guidance counsellor. Any who were university-bound usually reported finding these meetings helpful. For students planning to enter the workplace however, the benefits were not always evident. Once again, occupational choice tended to be the primary career concern. "What are you going to be?" was one of the most common questions heard by the young people of the day.

For the most part, happily, the transition from school to work was still relatively easy at the time. Jobs were plentiful. The economy was expanding. And the rather basic career and vocational guidance available was usually sufficient to help young people establish themselves in the Canadian workplace. For Morgan Parmenter however, there was clearly a gaping need in the Canadian school system for accurate career and vocational information. "He felt that students about to make a choice should have information about the world, about jobs and about themselves, about their strengths and weaknesses," recalls his widow, Eleanor.

Along with his occupational monographs and the range of psychological, aptitude and interest tests that had become more available after the Second World War, Parmenter distributed his own publications and the work of others through the Vocational Guidance Centre. He even set up a small publishing company to produce his books, *Success in the World of Work, You and Your Future and Exploring Occupations and Growing Up.*

As a hard working "idea" person, an educator turned teacher of teachers, Parmenter continued for the remainder of his career to try to fill what he saw as a large and growing need. But often he was a lone voice. "The Vocational Guidance Centre became his life's work," Eleanor Parmenter recalls. "He was there until he died in 1968."

Although guidance was still a relatively new and specialized area of education in Canada in Morgan Parmenter's day, it had been available in some schools in the United States since the early 1900s. For the first half of the century, the National Vocational Guidance Association in the United States had defined vocational guidance as "a process of assisting the individual to choose an occupation, prepare for it, enter upon it and progress in it."

The new psychology: A person-centered approach

Vocational guidance, like everything else in the newly prosperous post-war period, was affected by various general social trends. For instance, in the field of psychology and personal counselling, the trend was away from the study of behaviors and testing to what was to be called "client-centered" psychology, with a new focus on self-concept. Theories advanced by developmental psychologist Carl Rogers and famed psychoanalyst Erik Erikson had a dramatic impact on understandings of vocational guidance and counselling across North America. Also at this time, Abraham Maslow was gaining popularity as a motivation and personality theorist. Work like this contributed to the realization that people made not just one choice, but several throughout their work life.[2]

Redefining vocational guidance

This new definition placed the emphasis on the individual making a choice, rather than on the job that was chosen. For people involved in any kind of vocational guidance, it required a shift in approach. It meant moving from matching the individual to the job, to more client-centered techniques with a greater exploration of individual preferences and motivation.

In schools, the move to provide client-centered counselling had already begun. As introduced by Carl Rogers in the late 1940s, school counsellors had begun to be trained in this humanistic form of counselling and had become available to students.

Rogers was the first psychologist to advocate the importance of emotion and motivation on an individual's behaviour. The primary goals of therapy were self-acceptance and self-understanding. Though his theories evolved in the context of personal counselling, the shift which he advocated to adopt client-centred therapy led to a re-examination of the practice of testing human traits and matching them to job requirements.[3]

Developmental theories of psychology such as Erikson's eight-stage theory of development which suggested that humans have a number of psychosocial challenges that must be met before advancing to the next stage, influenced career counsellors to adopt a life stage approach.

This new focus on the individual and how he/she derived meaning from work was evident in Eugene A. Friedman and Robert J. Havighurst's 1954 book, *The Meaning of Work and Retirement* (Chicago Press). In it they outlined five ways in which work is meaningful: income, expenditure of time and energy, identification/status, association and as a source of meaningful life experiences.

Donald E. Super, a pioneering educator and career and vocational psychologist at that time, emphasized the psychological nature of career choice and the importance of self-concept in career counselling. His research also suggested that a career was developmental in nature and that vocational choice involved self and occupational understanding. Super said that vocational choice is a process rather than an event, vocation is a way of implementing a self-concept and that vocational maturity was defined in terms of five life-stages: growth, exploration, establishment, maintenance and decline.

Career counselling moves closer to applied psychology

These new theories in developmental psychology may have helped pave the way for career services to align further with the field of applied psychology. The new focus on the individual was applicable to career counselling as an exploration of the psychological dynamics involved in decision-making and studies of the process of development became understood as critical to the career development process.

The nature of career guidance expanded in concert with this focus on the individual. It was also stimulated by the growth in the economy. During the 1950s, education was more available, jobs were plentiful and individuals had more choices about where they would work—a new phenomenon for a century marked by two world wars and an economic depression of global magnitude.

Career counselling broadens

As a result, institutions across the country such as the Placement Centre at the University of Toronto and services offered by Ys in various communities, saw their client base steadily increasing. The U of T Placement Centre became concerned about the need for part-time jobs for older graduates and began moving toward representing men and women of all ages as well as all previous graduates. The Director of the Centre said, in making a placement, that "background experience, academic standing, personal tastes and other factors enter into each recommendation" for a job match.[4]

That definition changed significantly, however, when Donald Super suggested that vocational guidance should dwell less on the demands of the occupation under consideration and more on the skills, abilities and preferences of the individual. Super's theories were similar, in many ways, to the approach taken a few years earlier by Frank Lawson and Gerald Cosgrave when they focused the Toronto YMCA's Counselling Services procedures on the psychology of the individual.

By 1953, the YMCA was already reflecting this new approach to career counselling. A pamphlet, *The YMCA: 10 years of guidance: 1943-1953,* summarized their first ten years of guidance: "The Service aids people to choose vocations or courses of study and to manage their tasks in ways which lead to satisfaction, usefulness and progress. Assistance is based on careful study of the person. He is helped to understand himself, to assess his strengths and weaknesses and, in the light of this knowledge, discover how to apply his resources ably. There is no pressure, authority or criticism. Emphasis is on fitness as opposed to choosing a career for economic advantage alone. The Service has its foundation in the techniques of modern psychology."

The Y's expanded client base reflected a growing recognition of the need for career counseling throughout the life cycle: "People seek help at critical points throughout life such as entering courses of study, starting the first job, initial adjustment to work, settling into a permanent career, undertaking new responsibilities, encountering disappointments or difficulties, making job changes demanded by health or injury and tapering off as retirement approaches."

By this time, the Y had counselled over eight thousand people, assisted eighteen social agencies and government departments with vocational planning for persons in their care, and had five full-time, professionally trained psychologists on staff.

In 1953, the YMCA was also offering services for personnel planning to employers: "Tests are selected or designed for hiring, placement and advancement of employees. They may be administered by the employer or by the Counselling Service."

Hincks and Cosgrave also started to address career needs of older individuals by 1954, developing a course for people planning retirement through the YMCA. They organized a series of lectures delivered by authorities in public service, small business, arts studies and more, giving retirees a sense of "the horizons that beckon to people who have time to explore." The lectures were to show retired people how they could use their experiences to help others and find new, meaningful opportunities.

The struggle for professional legitimacy boosted through private philanthropy

Canada's small but growing career counselling field was still centred primarily in Toronto at the time, founded on the synergy between people like Frank Lawson, Gerald Cosgrave, Clarence Hincks and Morgan Parmenter. The focal point, in many ways, had been the YMCA. Since they had first opened in 1944, the Y's Counselling Service had welcomed some 12,400 people in search of aptitude testing and vocational guidance. In addition to the students, veterans, disabled workers and retired people being helped to redirect their working lives, a number of guidance teachers and placement and rehabilitation workers had been trained in the counselling techniques developed by Gerald Cosgrave.

From his perspective as chairman of the Toronto YMCA Counselling Service, Frank Lawson was equally aware of the growing need, although he took a somewhat different tack in his attempt to address it. "It became obvious that the problem was a lack of counsellors," he later recalled.

Initially focused on easing the transition for returning servicemen, Lawson had become increasingly concerned with the skills needed to appropriately counsel people in their career choices. He knew and believed in the value of work to a person's identity, but he also understood that the role of government would most likely always be to meet the needs of the market. There was an opportunity for private philanthropy to support the work that community-based agencies were able to deliver. Lawson was so committed to the field that, in 1959, he founded The Counselling Foundation of Canada.

Given the scope of the national need, Lawson was already pushing for a broader solution: Canadian universities needed to begin offering studies in applied psychology as well as experimental psychology. Until and unless that happened, he felt, the growing need for qualified counselling psychologists and better-trained personnel in schools and businesses would not be met within Canada. The YMCA Counselling Service itself needed counsellors, as there simply weren't enough around.

"We began to work with universities and tried to persuade them to set up counselling programs," he said. "But universities are creatures of tradition, they're large organizations and it takes a lot to affect change. Money was especially short. And if counselling programs were going to be set up, then other programs would have to be cut." As private philanthropy often does, The Counselling Foundation pointed the way for governments to consider the need for post-secondary institutions to provide not only career and placement counselling, but also academic support to the study and on-going development of the profession.

Although historically rather removed from the job search process of their graduates, the diversifying job market (where university grads found a wider choice for post-graduate employment) led some universities to become more open to seeing a role for themselves in this field. The University of Toronto established and funded a student placement centre in 1948. And because this centre worked closely with administration, the Students Administrative Council and the alumni association, a range of placement services for students was available shortly after the war; however, the extent to which faculty and university administrators embraced career counselling as a professional discipline worthy of further research and funding was very limited.

Early efforts were seen in the formation of the University Advisory Services which, in 1952, had become the University Counselling and Placement Association (UCPA) and was eventually broadened to become the Graduate Workforce Professions and later the Canadian Association of Career Educators and Employers (CACEE). With the growing number of student services on university and college campuses, a shift suggesting there was a difference between those people providing student services on campus and employer groups recruiting was beginning to take place. This facilitated the development of a new association known as the Canadian Association of College and University Student Services of which the Canadian University and College Counselling Association was a component.

By the turn of the next decade, following an initial rebuff from the University of Toronto, Lawson found a willing partner in Murray Ross, the pioneering president of the younger and less traditional York University. Together they formed the Counselling and Development Centre. What followed was an enormously successful funding partnership between the Foundation and the university sector across the country, to initially establish counselling centres on campus and to urge university curricula that supported the professional development of career counsellors in Canada.

Lawson was a proficient fundraiser, someone who got things done. Being of service to his community, and to young people growing up within it, had been a commitment of his since his own youth. Well-connected and aggressive, he believed that, "we find meaning in life through service." His example—coupled with his resources and willingness to carve out a new path—was to have a far-reaching effect on the development of the career counselling field into a profession.

Recession and skills shortages

In the minds of most Canadians however, a job was still a job. The prosperity of the post-war years had meant that almost anyone looking for work would have little trouble finding it.

On the country's centre stage, the Liberals had been in office since before the war, Quebec lawyer Louis St. Laurent having taken the helm when Mackenzie King retired in 1948. Together with the venerable C.D. Howe as his Minister of Trade and Commerce, "Uncle Louis" had inspired the confidence of voters and corporate employers alike with his sober and responsible management of Ottawa's affairs. Aside from a couple of brief economic downturns, his government had had the good fortune to preside over continued growth. In little more than a decade since the end of the war, the average industrial wage had doubled.

"High and stable levels of employment" had been one of Howe's key promises immediately following the war and for all intents and purposes he seemed to have delivered. Even the massive flood of immigrants from Europe, some one and a half million people between 1945 and 1957 alone, were readily absorbed into the workplace.

The widespread support enjoyed by the Liberals had waned considerably by the mid-1950s, however, and when his government invoked closure during a heated debate over a private gas pipeline, it bottomed out. Disillusioned by the temperamental scrapping among parliamentarians, Canadians were offended at the apparent arrogance of a government that had been in power for more than twenty years. A year later, in the 1957 election, the country shifted its support to the Conservatives, under leader John Diefenbaker.

National Archive of Canada

C. D. Howe, Time Magazine's "Man of the Year" 1952

The thrill of power notwithstanding, the Tory timing could not have been worse. Just a few months earlier, following on the heels of the United States, the country had slipped into the worst economic decline since 1945. Unemployment, which had remained in the 3 to 4 percent range for most of the decade, very nearly doubled. As manufacturing activity slowed, layoffs, plant closures and bankruptcies became common and the lengths of the lines of unemployed workers in Canadian cities grew.

It was recession with an added sting. For the first time since the end of the war, high unemployment and inflation reared their heads together, leaving the new government in a major quandary. Stimulating the economy to reduce unemployment would further fuel inflation, while tightening the purse strings to control inflation would increase unemployment.

The wind had shifted. With the Great Depression just twenty years behind them, Canadians could be forgiven for feeling nervous about the prospects of a return to hard times. Diefenbaker's government responded on several fronts, directing the Unemployment Insurance Commission to help people find work and introducing a "winter works program," Ottawa's first venture into the employment creation business since the Depression, other than veterans' programs.

Over the next few years, as it struggled to control the fallout, federal government spending would rise by 32 percent. One area to which it began to pay particular attention was the growing shortage of workplace skills. Although combined spending on vocational training was higher than ever before, Canada was still not producing enough trained workers to meet the needs of the labour market.

Published early in 1957, the report of the Liberal-appointed Royal Commission on Canada's Economic Prospects chaired by Walter Gordon highlighted the shortfall of skilled workers and recommended the establishment of new technical and vocational schools, as well as the expansion of existing facilities, at both secondary and post-secondary levels. Later that year, as it struggled to meet the immediate need, the Department of Labour also moved to head off the longer term implications spelled out by the report, offering a new Vocational and Technical Training Agreement to the provinces.

With the leading edge of the baby boom about to enter high school, the educational system was steadily expanding. The fact remained, however, that most Canadians job seekers were still very poorly educated, as many as half having failed to complete secondary school.

CLARENCE M. HINCKS

Problems finding a suitable path in the world of work have not always been recognized as such. Nor are people in need of direction necessarily able to articulate their difficulties clearly. Unless they are dealing with a sensitive and well-trained professional, they can just as easily be identified as misfits, slackers—even, on occasion, mentally unfit.

Fortunately for such people at least one sensitive, well-trained professional became active on their behalf, when Dr. Clarence Hincks began to pursue his particular interest in young people and their "mental hygiene," as it was called early in the 20th century.

Hincks' crusade for the cause of mental health became his life's work. For more than fifty years, he shone light where there had been none and championed the ways in which society could change not just its perceptions of mental health but its methods of treatment and prevention of mental disturbances.

Hincks was himself a survivor of mental illness. As a young man he had suffered from a deep and immobilizing depression. His subsequent recovery made a profound impression on him, proving from first hand experience that mental illness was not necessarily permanent.

He had studied medicine and, as a young physician in the early 20th century, was often called upon to examine "problem" school children. Some, he found, seemed inexplicably troubled, mirroring to him his own life experience. They weren't feeble minded, as was often assumed, but rather were suffering from depressive illness.

A telling opinion poll conducted by the Alberta Social Credit Party in 1956 found that one significant area where government action was seen to be needed was education. Among the many organizations, associations and chambers of commerce expressing their concerns was the Canadian Petroleum Association, which urged "a reduction in pupil-teacher ratios in classrooms, more and better qualified teachers, better materials of instruction" and greater efforts to equip young people for "job efficiency in the age of machines."

Growing integration with the U.S. economy and ongoing retooling

In industrial communities across the country, workers attempting to enter or re-enter the labour market were hard-pressed to obtain the training they needed if their skills were not up to date. Probably nobody made the point better than a Windsor, Ontario unemployment insurance official who pointed out at the time that many of the thousands of workers who had been laid off from the auto industry would never work in it again.

"They will never again build autos," he said, "because their jobs are gone. Machines have taken over their jobs. They are, in effect, the possessors of outmoded skills and no doubt history will categorize them with the village smithy, the old lamplighter and many, many others."[5]

Nor was the outdated worker alone. Whole industries were running into similar problems as the pace of economic and technological change quickened. The Royal Commission Report on Canada's Economic

At a medical meeting in Buffalo, New York in 1913, Hincks came across a book that would ultimately change the direction of his life. Written by a young American engineer, Clifford Beers, it recounted Beers' own two-year depressive illness and subsequent recovery. The book and its author had been instrumental in the formation of an early mental hygiene movement in the U.S. Both inspired Hincks to begin a similar movement in Canada in 1918. The organization he founded is well known today as the Canadian Mental Health Association.

Hincks' ability to enlighten and educate people to the true nature of mental illness was to play a catalytic role in the evolution of vocational guidance in Canada. He believed that work—appropriate and suitable work—could help young people resolve some of the problems they encountered. He encouraged Toronto educator Morgan Parmenter to publish and distribute information about occupations and workplace opportunities.

And while the country was still at war, he approached the YMCA and found that some of his ideas meshed with that organization's growing concerns about the pressing employment needs of young men. Vocational guidance, Hincks told the YMCA Board of Governors, would help many young men, some of whom were ending up in Canada's mental institutions simply because they had nowhere else to go.

The Toronto YMCA Counselling Service was established in 1943, another victory for Hincks' crusade and a pivotal moment in the growth and application of vocational counselling as a critical component in successful and fruitful lives.

Prospects had also stressed the growing problems caused by "Americanization" of the economy and urged the government to exercise tighter control over foreign investment.

It was a clear indication of how heavily Canada's economic well-being had come to depend on U.S. dollars. The old bonds with Britain had been weakening steadily and exports to other countries had also declined while Canada/U.S. trade grew. Roughly three quarters of foreign investment in Canada now came from the United States and the U.S. was Canada's largest export customer, consuming roughly two thirds of Canada's goods. The British, on the other hand, were now responsible for only 15 percent of Canada's foreign investments.

> "No other country in the world with something like our relative state of development has ever had such a degree of foreign domination. Canada is being pushed down the road that leads to loss of any effective power to be masters in our own household."
>
> James Coyne, President of Bank of Canada, to Canadian Chamber of Commerce, 1960

In the workplace, the costs of this ongoing realignment were becoming increasingly visible, as the heavy industries established in times of war declined. Perhaps it was inevitable, in a country of fifteen million people perched on the border of a colossus ten times its size. Or perhaps, as historian Desmond Morton suggests, in his book *Working People*, Canadians were just not resourceful enough and feeling a bit too comfortable to care.

"Perhaps by ingenuity and hard work, Canada might have built herself a permanent lead. Instead she built on the large short-term benefits of her 'special relationship' with the United States. One by one the technological gains Canadians had built for themselves in wartime industries vanished. Shipbuilding was gone by 1950. The aircraft industry, electronics and communications followed. Canada was returning to her old dependence on the raw materials her people pulled from the ground."

Twenty years after it began, the wartime industrial juggernaut was feeling its age. It would rise again soon enough, albeit in a new, less independent guise. In the uncertain light of the late '50s, however, it looked anything but robust. And the emerging interconnectedness of the North American economies would pose challenges to the career counselling community in Canada, which aspired to form its own professional identity.

[1] Craig Brown, ed. *History of Canada* (Toronto: Key Porter, 2000).
[2] Edwin Herr, "Career Counselling: a process in process". *British Journal of Guidance & Counselling*, Vol 25, No 1, 1997.
[3] Zunker, Vernon G., *Career Counselling: Applied Concepts of Life Planning* (Brooks-Cole Publishing, 1998).
[4] "Placement Service Puts the Right Man in the Right Job," *Varsity Graduate*, Vol 3 No 4, May 1950.
[5] "Education and Training for the Unemployed" *Labour Gazette*, 1959, pp. 1154 – cited in John Hunter's book, 138.

CHAPTER 6

A VOLATILE
Economy
AND AN
Expectation
THAT
GOVERNMENT
COULD DO IT ALL

"No Unemployment Crisis?" asked the headline in the *Toronto Daily Star*. "Signs are that at the bottom of the employment cycle this winter there will be 600,000 or more jobless. What is this, if not a national emergency?"

As it turned out, a national emergency it was not. But unemployment had scarcely been worth a newspaper's attention for twenty years or more and now, in 1960, it was cropping up on editorial pages. "The puzzling and disappointing attitude of the Diefenbaker administration toward the unemployment situation thus far has been uninspired," is the way *The Ottawa Citizen* put it. "No one expects Mr. Diefenbaker to eliminate unemployment. But Canadians have a right to expect leadership and action on the unemployment issue, rather than the 'let's hope it goes away' attitude that has been a characteristic of this government."

There had been about seven recessions since the century began, the most devastating, of course, the Great Depression. And every time the economy faltered, whatever the issues of the moment, the attentions of government, the media and society at large were drawn anew to the plight of the unemployed.

In 1961, the unemployment index hit a postwar high of 7.1 percent and anxiety rippled across the country. The jobless numbers had been climbing since 1959 and the layoffs occurring throughout the industrial sector made it clear that the long-playing record of post-war growth was beginning to show some cracks.

Already beleaguered by federal-provincial relations, issues of Quebec representation and nuclear defense, the Diefenbaker government was under intense pressure to do something about the growing numbers of unemployed.

The winter works programs introduced in 1957 were continued and expanded. Restrictions on immigration, implemented at the same time, were extended as well.

"Is unemployment here to stay?"

Something in the nature of unemployment appeared to be changing and among the factors contributing to this were the very programs the federal government had charged with providing a solution.

Such, at least, was the hypothesis put forward in an influential magazine article, published in 1959 just as the economy was recovering from one recession and about to head into another. Written by Blair Fraser, a respected *Maclean's* magazine editor, the article questioned the government's ability to uphold its post-war commitment to "high and stable employment and income."

In what seems to have been the first comment of its kind in the popular press, Fraser pointed a finger at government interventions and, in particular, unemployment insurance. It had a negative impact on the functioning of the labour market, he said. "Is Unemployment Here to Stay?" the article asked. And the simple answer, in Fraser's view, appeared to be yes.

Quoting unnamed "government economists," Fraser made the case that Ottawa's employment and income policy had worked fairly well until recently, but the high levels of both inflation and unemployment witnessed during the recession of 1957-58 were something new. "They think that in good times or bad we shall have more unemployment than we've been used to having," he wrote, "and enough to make it a serious national problem."

"Abuses" of unemployment insurance were at the heart of Fraser's critique, abuses and the attitudes that led to them. Some workers welcomed unemployment as "UI-paid vacations," he said. "Fishermen who were paid for winter months when they would not normally have worked, workers who would only take a job if it was in their own trade and their own town." It was of little importance whether or not such "abuses" could be justified. By upping the cost of the UI program and slowing down placements, they were inhibiting the capacity of the economy to adapt to changing conditions.

"Structural unemployment" was the name given to this new phenomenon in a report from the Special Senate Committee on Manpower and Employment that was submitted in 1961. Slower economic growth during a recessionary period certainly had contributed to the growing numbers of jobless, the report said. Other factors such as sectoral layoffs and declining exports had had an effect, as well.

Still, the committee noted, these concerns could not account for the entire problem: "The post-war era has been a period of accelerating technological progress, of rapid innovation, of revolutionary improvements in labour-saving devices, and of pronounced shifts in the growth of consumer demand. These far-ranging changes have necessitated a general upgrading in human skills, large-scale movements between occupations, and a high degree of mobility of labour between industries and between geographical areas. The economy and its manpower have failed to adjust to these basic developments on a sufficient scale or with sufficient speed."

Fitting the man to the job was getting more complicated all the time.

Manpower utilization vs. human resource development

In 1963, however, the economy resumed its growth and the woes of the workforce began to subside but not soon enough to turn the tide of growing disillusionment in the Diefenbaker government's lackluster management of the economy. Although a strong orator with pockets of intense popular support, Diefenbaker proved to be an indecisive leader and struggled to preside over a fractured caucus. In the election that followed, the Tories' fate was sealed.

For the Liberals, it was a modest victory at best, resulting in a minority government. In rejecting the Conservatives, Canadians had voted, above all else, for prosperity. Ironically, as Prime Minister Lester B. Pearson took office, the economy was already on the mend.

As the economy returned to health, most of the unemployed returned to work and the unemployment index dropped back down below 4 percent. Concerns about structural unemployment did not go away, however. Echoing a Royal Commission a few years earlier on Canada's Economic Prospects, these concerns surfaced in the press: "A skill squeeze has caught up with Canada," was how *The Financial Post* put it in a feature article on November 7, 1964. "Jobs are available now," it went on, "but the men are not and shortages are reported through the skill scale from tradesmen to professionals."

Business was suffering, according to corporate employers who complained that they couldn't find the skilled workers they needed. "Good jobs are going begging, but the unemployed can't fill them," the article said, citing estimates that only 7 percent of the Canadian workforce had secondary schooling or better. Over 40 percent, according to the same estimates, had not even finished primary school.

Most needed were workers with technical skills, people able to work as machinists, toolmakers, mechanics and repairmen. Service skills were in demand, as well, the article said, in sales and clerical positions.

In the 1960s, shortages of skilled workers and workers willing to accept low skilled jobs led to the gradual removal of race restrictions that had always been part of Canada's immigration policy. Resentment grew from the perception that immigrants took jobs that Canadian-born job seekers lacked qualifications to fill. Closer to the root of the problem was the fact that public policies created few training programs in emerging occupations and Canadians were given too little information about the programs that did exist. There was also the tricky problem of enticing high school graduates to consider further education when high-paying jobs in manufacturing, construction and resource extraction were available to them.

Governments, it was widely believed, had a social responsibility, even a moral obligation, to provide some form of assistance to Canadians who found themselves at a disadvantage in the workplace. Since the Second World War, in fact, the federal government had been playing an increasingly important supporting role in a common federal-provincial-territorial objective of human resource development.

The Gordon Commission in 1957 had highlighted the growing concerns over workplace skills and forecasted the shortages that were now beginning to appear, proposing as a remedy the expansion of existing secondary technical and vocational schools and the development of new ones. It had argued as well for more post-secondary schools with continuing education programs for part-time study, recognizing that adults as well as young people would be customers for such services.

The Diefenbaker government had taken the report seriously and, despite heated exchanges in the House of Commons, the legislation that would revolutionize the country's post-secondary training system had passed unanimously in December of 1960.

The Technical and Vocational Training Assistance Act covered nine different programs, representing a complex mix of training directives and incentives that became program development streams. Curricula and programming were developed to address the training needs of unemployed adults, students, people with disabilities, members of the armed forces and people needing to upgrade their skills in order to move ahead in their careers.

Massive amounts of money were allocated to shared cost agreements between Ottawa and the provinces. By 1965, the federal government's commitments amounted to roughly $470 million, creating over one hundred thousand "training spaces."

Education without adequate guidance

Throughout these years, in ever increasing numbers, the baby boom continued its advance. For the field of education it was a sea change, as wave after wave of young people poured into Canada's high schools, heavily influenced by a new generation of parents who believed that higher education would pave the way to more satisfying employment and future success.

School and college building activity across the country became so intense that every day during 1962 and 1963 a new school opened somewhere in the country. New opportunities also opened up for teachers, professors, instructors…and for counsellors. By the middle of the decade, more than a million young people were little more than a year away from the day when most of them would begin knocking on doors throughout the industrialized workplace.

Programs to help young people manage the school-to-work transition had challenged Frank Parsons in the early days of the century when he first articulated a definition of vocational guidance. It was the same challenge Morgan Parmenter had taken on in the 1940s, when he created the Vocational Guidance Centre and began teaching guidance at the Ontario College of Education.

Thanks in large part to the efforts of a far-sighted few—Parmenter in particular and his successor, Carl Bedal—a certain amount of guidance training, materials and other information had been made available to Canadian teachers. Since 1945, Parmenter's journal, *Guidance & Counselling*, had been distributed widely.

As the '60s advanced, however, life and work grew more complicated making effective guidance counselling even more important. Nonetheless, as indicated in a survey of Canadian schools in the '60s, the guidance services offered were for the most part woefully inadequate, especially when it came to helping young people make work and career decisions.

In part, it was a simple problem of workload and available time. According to Parmenter, a ratio of two hundred students to one guidance teacher could be considered reasonable. In practice, however, the ratio was often more like six hundred to one. In some schools, a single guidance teacher might be expected to deal with the needs of as many as eight hundred students.

Beyond concerns of numbers, there was also the question of expertise. Few teachers, it seemed, had had the benefit of experience beyond the world of academia and had little exposure to the broader world of work. Guidance in general, and career or vocational guidance in particular, was generally held in lower esteem than other teaching duties and often passed to the youngest and least experienced teachers. Nor were there many educational opportunities for those interested in this specialized area of education. In many Canadian provinces it was not even a requirement that guidance teachers have specific training.

For all the attention it paid to one essential need—fundamental knowledge of academic and vocational skills—the educational system was neglecting another—the need for direction in the workplace where these academic and vocational skills would most commonly be applied. What was necessary, clearly, were comprehensive policies, improved procedures and more training of teachers. Few were more vocal in making this case than Frank Lawson and Gerald Cosgrave.

"Counselling for teenagers and adults would not be so greatly necessary if better trained teachers were available in the elementary school system," Lawson wrote at the time. Emphasizing the widespread failure of universities to establish programs in counselling psychology, the chairman of the Toronto YMCA Counselling Service noted that, "many of our counselling psychologists in recent years have had to be imported, which is certainly a reflection on all of our university psychology departments."[1]

Deeply concerned about the lack of counselling available to young people to plan their working lives, Lawson strongly supported an Ontario Select Committee Report which called for "cradle to grave" counselling and argued that, "the importance of vocational guidance is increasing at every level in our educational and training system."[2]

"We're encouraging an appalling waste of manpower," Lawson said. "About 75 percent of high school youngsters don't know what they want in life and many end up in university who shouldn't be there at all."

In its attempts to take up some of the slack, the Toronto YMCA Counselling Service was providing counselling for some seven to eight hundred clients a year and turning away another two for every person they saw. "Organizations such as ours are providing emergency services," Gerald Cosgrave pointed out. "Schools should be providing regular psychological testing and counselling from the elementary level right up through technical colleges and universities."

In 1965, Lawson persuaded Gerald Cosgrave to join The Counselling Foundation of Canada as Director of Counselling (CFC), to support his campaign to convince university presidents and planners to establish programs in counselling psychology.

Draft dodgers and the dawn of the communications age

University presidents and planners had plenty on their own agendas, of course. The '60s were hectic years on campuses throughout North America, as radical groups of protesting students challenged social values on everything from civil rights to the Vietnam War.

Canada became a haven for Americans fleeing the draft and the images of dissent and "flower power" in Berkeley and Haight-Ashbury found their way north of the border as well. A very different generation was beginning to emerge and the differences were becoming more acute as the new generation gained university age.

This was the dawn of the Age of Communications and the pace of change was ratcheted up another notch by the expansion of telecommunications. Vast networks of connectivity were being formed and, in a very few years, all parts of the world would be linked by telephones, satellites and computers.

It was the start of the Television Age and the Canadian Broadcasting Corporation had the longest network in the world. The Alouette communications satellite was launched in 1962, making Canada the third nation in space. The globe had become a village and University of Toronto communications guru Marshall McLuhan alerted the world to the message in the medium.

During the 1960s and '70s, Canada saw an influx of American young people, who like thier Canadian counterparts, formed a new generation of "seekers" of jobs and a better world.

CP Picture Archive

The country's automotive industry, centred in Ontario, sent out multiple shoots, reshaping the industrial heartland. General Motors was building its one hundred millionth car and Alberta's oil patch was on a roll. And in Montreal, there was a construction boom as Quebec prepared for Expo '67.

With manufacturing in full swing, jobs were plentiful and Canadians were more optimistic. Spurred by the renewed flush of prosperity, shoppers began to expect a full range of products on store shelves and consumerism emerged as a powerful economic engine. While many of the products in demand were imported, some originated in Canada, providing jobs in the factories where they were manufactured.

Indeed, as the service sector grew, a very different set of needs began to dominate employers' conceptions of the ideal employee. There were fewer entry-level, low-skilled, machine-oriented jobs available and more sales and clerical positions were in need of workers. Despite evidence of the future importance of service sector employment, however, only 1 percent of students was enrolled in training for service occupations.

An active manpower policy

Throughout these years, the expansion of government services contributed significantly to the growth of the service economy. Since the Great Depression, in slow, incremental ways, governments, both federal and provincial, had become more involved in the fabric of Canadian life.

Jurisdictional concerns complicated matters, as always. However, "there was a clear public demand for a 'Canadian' approach to problems," writes veteran pollster Angus Reid. And because the provinces welcomed federal funding, many overlapping programs were developed.

"There were plans to encourage investment in Canadian stocks," Reid continues, "to discourage foreign ownership, to encourage Canadian culture, to encourage investment in the Atlantic provinces, to discourage pollution of the Great Lakes, to encourage participation in sports, to discourage smoking, to encourage cross-cultural exchanges with Quebec, to discourage hateful attitudes toward minority ethnic groups, to encourage the development of nations on the other side of the world. Everywhere you looked, it seemed, another government department had drafted another ambitious program."[3]

Of course, as Reid points out, "all these plans required platoons of bureaucrats to implement them." The opportunities seemed limitless.

A new sense of mission fueled the partnership between Canadians and their governments, a revival of the "can do" attitude that had brought Canada through the Depression and the war. Now Canadians had the money to do it. "This was the decade of universal medicare. Workers were given a new sense of security in the form of the Canada Pension Plan. There were social assistance programs, low-interest loans for students in post-secondary education, low-cost housing programs. And for rural or depressed communities in poorer regions, there was money to develop local resources and create opportunities."[4]

Government was also far more involved in the labour market. Employment policies and programs were implemented. Adjustment programs were initiated for displaced workers. Grants and loans were made available to workers who had to move to find employment.

Several hundred new employees were hired to work as Manpower Counsellors, many of them recent university graduates in the social sciences. "Their task was to help people, whether unemployed or unsatisfactorily employed, to obtain the employment that was likely to maximize their lifetime earnings," according to Tom Kent, the deputy minister at the time. Although matching workers with employers—job placement—

remained their primary goal, "this required much more than information about the existing employment opportunities in the area. It required counselling skills. It required understanding of the abilities and experience needed for various occupations."

Such sentiments notwithstanding, more than a decade would pass before government counsellors such as these would be specifically trained in counselling techniques.

[1] Correspondence with *Globe and Mail* reporter Barry Zwicker, October 28, 1966.
[2] "Vocational Counseling Becoming Lifetime Aid" – *Financial Post*, July 13, 1963.
[3] Angus Reid, "Shakedown: How the New Economy is Changing our Lives."
[4] Alvin Finkel and Margaret Conrad, *History of the Canadian Peoples* (Don Mills: Pearson Education).

CHAPTER 7

AN EMERGING
Profession
AND THE
Growth
OF THE
NOT-FOR-PROFIT
SECTOR

In 1961, the Economic Council of Canada had calculated that near-ly 30 percent of Canadians earned incomes low enough to qualify them as poor. Billions of federal and provincial dollars were fun-neled into regional development programs involving subsidies to businesses that established in impoverished areas, often with less than impressive results. From a forestry complex in northern Manitoba, to a heavy water plant in Cape Breton to New Brunswick's notorious Bricklin auto maker, there were numerous examples of failed giveaways that left holes in the public purse.

With the objective of helping disadvantaged workers in the expan-sive mood of the '60s, the Pearson government stole an idea from Lyndon Johnson and decided to wage a War on Poverty. One campaign in that war would have far-reaching implications for career counselling in Canada. The man who came up with the idea was a relative new-comer to the federal government, a man with a diverse background in psychological counselling, training, human resources and business by the name of Stuart Conger.

In many ways, Conger represented a new breed in the evolving field of workplace counselling—the professional who crossed the sectoral divides, applying expertise gained in one context to problems in quite another and in the process bringing about a cross-fertilization that ulti-mately benefited the field as a whole. He was an idea man, committed to seeing that career guidance infiltrated as many operations as possible.

From his early work as a rehabilitation psychologist, Conger had opted to work in the private sector. For a decade, he worked for organi-zations such as Canadian General Electric, as a counsellor in its per-sonnel assessment program; and Ontario Hydro, in human resources training. Early in the 1960s, he joined the Department of Trade and Commerce to set up a national small business training program.

In 1965, Conger's training program had been absorbed into the Department of Labour and Ross Ford, Director of the Technical and Vocational Branch in the department, invited Conger to throw a few of his ideas into the hat.

S. Conger

"He asked me to work up some programs for the War on Poverty," Conger recalls. "He asked me to set up a task force, which I did. We looked at a number of things going on in the States, in the war on poverty there, and made a number of proposals." The one that caught the attention of Ford and the others in the Technical and Vocational Branch was a program called Canada NewStart. From the outset, it was a fish from a different kettle, a quirky departure from bureaucratic business as usual. It had been designed "to test innovative ways of improving the use of the labour force and reducing poverty in selected areas" while exercising a certain degree of "flexibility and autonomy from established procedures" in the process.

The idea, says Conger, was to set up a series of experimental laboratories across the country "to invent new methods of counselling and training adults who were disadvantaged as to their educational level." Many of these people had neither the necessary skills to work in new jobs being created nor the problem-solving skills needed to maintain them.

Despite the appeal and the unique approach implicit in his idea, Conger's superiors were all too aware that it would never be accepted unless it could somehow work within the framework of Canada's complex federal-provincial relations. Conger , with unprecedented success, would implement what had since 1913 been the federal government's perception of federal/provincial collaboration. After a year of negotiations with the provinces, NewStart Programs were set up in six provinces: Alberta, Saskatchewan, Manitoba, New Brunswick, PEI and Nova Scotia. Each was given an initial grant of $100,000, then further funding for a period of five years. "Each had a different set of projects," according to Conger, "although some were overlapping."

Of the products and initiatives generated in the NewStart "laboratories," several outlived the five-year program. From NewStart Nova Scotia came DACUM, a competency-based training curriculum development model that has since been adopted by educators worldwide. And from Saskatchewan came curricula for literacy and career planning, individualized learning programs, a recreational program designed to teach English as a second language and the enormously successful Life Skills program, originally conceived in New York under the U.S. anti-poverty program, Training for Youth.

The workplace was becoming ever more complicated, an arena of many converging and competing interests. In many different ways, behind the scenes, in small pockets of regional activity such as those of Canada NewStart, the federal government was becoming much more active in addressing workplace needs. Somewhere in the innards of Parliament Hill, a decision had been taken, a responsibility had been accepted for the development of the country's human capital.

Aware of Conger's background in guidance, Ross Ford asked him to look into vocational counselling. He was especially concerned, Conger says, about the lack of career guidance Canadian students received in high school. Ford told Conger of an extensive study currently underway. The provincial Departments of Education and the federal Department of Labour had combined their efforts to survey some one hundred and fifty thousand students in close to four hundred secondary schools across the country. Raymond Breton from the University of Toronto had been commissioned to write the final report.

The study indicated that most high school students had no idea what they were going to do the day they left school, Conger recalls. "We need a national position paper on career guidance in technical and vocational education," Ford told him. "Can you put a team together and do one?"

Conger approached Gerald Cosgrave, newly appointed as Counselling Director of The Counselling Foundation of Canada. Conger remembered the work Cosgrave had contributed to the Canadian General Electric personnel assessment unit and asked him to sit on the committee and author the report. *Educational and Vocational Guidance in Technical and Vocational Education* by Gerald P. Cosgrave was widely distributed in 1965 to support guidance services and build awareness of the need to serve the Canadian labour market.

The report recommended the development of initiatives to enhance a student's understanding of their own skills, interests and competencies, and the development of a personal plan to gain the further education and training the student required. The report also noted that a twenty-minute interview with a guidance counsellor every year or so wasn't sufficient to meet an individual student's guidance needs.

It proved to be a provocative document. Some high-school guidance counsellors saw it as threatening, or at least critical of their efforts. They turned out in large numbers to the founding meeting of the Canadian Guidance Counsellors Association (CGCA) at which Cosgrave was a speaker.

"For some incomprehensible reason, the guidance counsellors took that report as a reflection that they weren't doing a proper job and were very angry about it," says Conger. Cosgrave, who Conger remembers as "a very gentle man," was both shocked and astounded by their antagonism." But the good thing was it bought a lot of counsellors to the founding meeting of the association and got it off to a good start," says Conger.

In 1965 the YMCA had launched a Counselling Service Practicum and support course for university students, upon which in due course various universities would fashion their own undergraduate, graduate and doctoral programs. This had met with tremendous resistance though, as each sector ducked any potential role they might play, preferring to suggest that someone else – like school boards or the newly created community college networks – should take this on.

Also in 1965 the Canadian Guidance Counselling Association was formed. This professional body began as an informal networking organization of teachers providing guidance services in schools. The CGCA became an avid participant in the early NATCON events influenced by the emerging sense of community and shared identity forming within the career counselling field. Today, this organization is known as the Canadian Counselling Association (CCA).

Choosing partners

In 1970, Stuart Conger was in Prince Albert, Saskatchewan, having taken over as Director of the Training and Research Development Station (TRANS) previously known as the Saskatchewan NewStart Program.

In the spirit of his innovative program, Conger had decided to pursue a special interest of his own. Life skills training had captured his attention because it provided a concept of teaching people to be competent in managing their own lives and, under his direction, a Life Skills division was established.

Dr. Winthrop Adkins and Dr. Sidney Rosenberg, the American creators of the Life Skills concept, had been invited to come to Canada to spend six weeks with the Saskatchewan course writers, coaches and researchers, out of which had come a second generation of Life Skills lessons.

Over three years, the Saskatchewan Life Skills team devoted forty person years and half a million dollars to the development of their new, improved model of the curriculum, designed to teach problem-solving skills and the management of life in such areas as self, family, use of leisure time and work.

Aware that a Toronto branch of the YWCA hoped to pilot a Life Skills project for women with low levels of education, Conger turned once again to the CFC's Gerald Cosgrave, this time to ask for his support for the development of a new program.

"It would appear that the Department of Manpower and Immigration is prepared to fund the development of new counselling methods (for both youths and adults)," Conger wrote. "But it can fund the use of the methods only in adult training programs. Presumably the schools can do the same for in-school youth. The gap then, is for women who are planning to re-enter the labour force and for men and women who are now in the labour force but need and want better vocational guidance...for these people, there is not only a lack of a good guidance program, but also the lack of a delivery system."

It was Conger's proposal that the Counselling Foundation of Canada play a unique funding role to help bring the Life Skills program to the public. TRANS would train YWCA personnel in the Life Skills process and in turn the CFC agreed to provide a grant to the YWCA to create the Life Skills program for single mothers as a pilot project. An extensive Life Skills manual was created as well, the first of a series of such manuals that would support a "life-skills movement" in the counselling field that continues to this day.

Perhaps the most significant contribution of the Life Skills program was its affirmation, perhaps for the first time in "official" circles, of the whole person as part of the vocational counselling process. Through the efforts of the YWCA and the TRANS team, the abstract, so-called "soft" skills that people need to manage their lives and their careers were recognized as important to an individual's chances of career success.

The changing workforce

The '60s and '70s ushered in other social developments which had a tremendous impact on the workforce. Initially during the immediate post-war period, European refugees and immigrants arrived in Canada and formed close-knit support communities through which they adapted to Canadian life and found work. Gathering principally in the larger cities where family members may have preceded them, some of these networks were informal; others were organized by culture. For example, in 1961 the Centre Organizzativo Scuole Techniche Italiane (COSTI) formed to help place skilled tradespeople, originally from southern Europe, into the burgeoning construction industry. Using immigrant labour was a tradition in Canada, where both railroads had been built with the assistance of workers of primarily Asian origin. But the labour market of the latter part of the century proved to be more volatile as did the adjustment needs of arriving workers. Agencies like these formed across the country; for example, the United Chinese Community Service (Vancouver, 1973); and Employment Services for Immigrant Women (Toronto, 1978). In the 1980s, COSTI went on to merge with the Italian Immigrant Aid Society, thereby becoming the country's largest career and employment agency serving immigrants.

Of course, the other startling change to the Canadian workforce of the '60s and '70s was the addition of thousands of women who, having won their equality rights some fifty years before, were now liberated from the confines of motherhood and encouraged by the popular culture to have a career too! The injection of female workers was to have a tremendous impact on the Canadian workplace. In government and community-based programs, women became what was then called a "target group," meaning that specialized career counselling services would be provided to ease their transition into the labour market.

Another group that became an obvious priority for government and agency career counselling programs were people of aboriginal descent— or First Nations as they would eventually choose to be referred. Marginalized by decades of government policy which disenfranchised First Nations from their land and way of life, by the 1970s Canadians and their governments had come to realize that First Nations' people would require very specialized career counselling to assist their entry into the labour market. For the most part, these specialized counselling programs were developed by First Nations' communities themselves, with support from government, corporate sponsors, and/or private philanthropy.

Labour market information and technology

Equally important to an individual's success, suggested employment policy pioneer Bryce Stewart, when he put forward his vision of the National Employment Service, was accurate educational and occupational information. Not until the 1970s, however, would a branch of the federal government, the Manpower Information and Analysis Branch, be equipped to provide comprehensive labour-market information.

Just as the development of tests and psychometric assessments had advanced the field in the years following the Second World War, the development of quality sources of information advanced it even further. Publications and assessment tools were produced by the department including The Canadian Occupational Forecast and Occupational Monographs and the Canadian Classification And Dictionary Of Occupations (CCDO). While specific to Canadian requirements, the government's earliest productions of this kind were adapted from American products, especially the U.S. Department of Labour's Dictionary of Occupational Titles.

Many of the products and initiatives produced by this department were targeted to young people and distributed through Canada Manpower Centres. Nudging into provincial jurisdiction, they were also made available to high schools across the country. Most teachers, struggling to keep up with changing requirements, were happy to receive them, as there were few Canadian career resources available at the time.

That would soon change. Increasing levels of unemployment, growing concern about the lack of career planning among Canadian youth and employers' complaints about shortages of skilled workers were beginning to have an impact.

The fledgling field of career counselling and development had begun to find a place in the Canadian labour market initiatives of the federal government. In its inimitable way, Ottawa had been planting seeds and some of them ultimately bore fruit. Career and labour market information was being collected and published. Career materials and products were being created. New partnerships were being forged to deliver these to the people who needed them.

The human potential movement

During the 1960s, we saw further evolution in psychology. There was an increased emphasis on existential and humanistic theories and people were looking for meaning in their lives. This became known as the human potential movement, which was reflected in career counselling as an emphasis on achieving a greater awareness of one's experiences and potential, thus increasing one's chances for self-assertion and self-direction. Accompanying this shift was increased research on motivation and personality within psychology, together with a greater emphasis on self-assessment and encouragement of the individual to find work that would be personally meaningful.

Training professionals for the field

As the needs became more obvious and the field began to grow, the lack of specific training for counsellors continued to be a matter of concern for many, including both Gerald Cosgrave and Frank Lawson. Graduate studies in vocational guidance and counselling were still rare in English Canada in the early 1960s.

A few guidance teachers and a number of placement and rehabilitation workers had made arrangements to study under Cosgrave in his years with the YMCA's Counselling Service. Other teachers had attended Morgan Parmenter's summer courses in guidance at the Ontario College of Education in Toronto.

Graduate studies in educational counselling or psychology were available in the United States at the time, recalls Myrne Nevison. In 1960, Nevison, who had been a Burnaby, B.C. guidance teacher, moved to the U.S. to attend the University of Minnesota where she earned both an M.A. and a Ph.D. in educational psychology.

"The Cold War was underway at the time and the American government had put money into educational psychology to ensure that American children received proper counselling so they could fight the Russians," she recalls with a chuckle. "I guess Canadian politicians didn't worry about such things."

In Canada, specialized courses and programs in advanced psychology began to slowly appear in the 1960s to address a growing demand for longer and more careful preparation of the nation's teachers. While a year of Normal School was adequate teacher preparation in the 1950s, by the mid-1960s, school boards, particularly in urban areas, were insisting that prospective educators have full university degrees.

In 1965, in Ontario, the Toronto YMCA had launched a Counselling Service Practicum for university students and began offering a course to counsellors called "A Sound Academic Introduction to Theory and Technical Aspects of the Counselling Process." Neither the practicum nor the course were greeted with much enthusiasm by Ontario educators, however. Education of this kind, it was generally believed at the time, should be offered within the traditional educational system, either at universities, in the new Colleges of Applied Arts and Technology, or in-house by local school boards. F. J. Clute, Ontario's Assistant Superintendent, Curriculum Section (Guidance), stated his objections in a letter to the YMCA in 1967:

"I am less happy about your proposed counsellor training course… In the Ontario system, only teachers with at least one hundred hours of instruction are able to assume scheduled counselling duties in the schools…with the advent of the Colleges of Applied Arts and Technology, with the increase in the number of available extension courses provided by the universities, and with the establishment of in-service courses by local school boards, there would appear to be plenty of recognized training institutions to set up necessary courses for prospective counsellors."

Such feelings notwithstanding, it would be many years before professional development for vocational or employment counsellors would become readily available in Ontario's post-secondary educational system.

Ultimately, as it turned out, the YMCA practicum would be used by under- and post-graduate students from York University in Toronto, McGill University in Montreal and Waterloo University in Waterloo, Ontario, as well as Toronto's Ontario Institute for Studies in Education.

The Counselling Foundation of Canada continued to promote post-secondary educational programs in applied psychology. Ultimately, more than twenty Canadian universities would benefit from Counselling Foundation grants to support the teaching of applied psychology and improve the quality of counselling services and educational programs.

In 1965, Myrne Nevison returned to British Columbia to become an Associate Professor of Education at the University of British Columbia, where she initiated a graduate program in educational psychology, the first in western Canada. In Montreal, McGill University began studies in educational psychology about the same time; interestingly, francophone educators in Quebec had had a three-year program in career counselling at Laval University since 1950.

At the University of Victoria, a graduate program was introduced in the 1970s. Vance Peavy, who would go on to become one of the field's best known theorists, had recently arrived at the University, migrating north from Oregon.

In his earliest days at U Vic, as it is affectionately known, Peavy found not a single course in counselling. He sought and won the approval of the University of Victoria's academic board to begin building courses in educational counselling into the curriculum. A graduate program for a master's degree in counselling followed. Peavy also established a Counselling Centre for the university's student population. And ultimately, he added a Ph.D. in counselling to the university's offerings.

Those interested in teaching careers sometimes took a diploma in education after completing another degree; however, in the 1970s, four-year teaching degrees became more common. The teaching faculty in these programs, generally younger educators themselves with advanced degrees, proved to be open to establishing new fields and approaches. Enrollment in these faculties grew rapidly as those with education as a specific career goal began to increase the number of years they studied educational theory and practice.

Liberation, revolution and the hidden costs of a "grant boom"

The frenzy for Prime Minister Pierre Elliot Trudeau, was called Trudeaumania.

CP Picture Archive (Peter Bregg)

If the contrary inclinations of youth were a wakeup call for educators in the '60s, by the time the '70s rolled around they had begun to challenge the entire society. The leading edge of the boomer wave began to spill out of high schools, colleges and universities, and thousands of young people flooded into Canada's cities in search of work.

For the most part, Canadians and their governments were still in an optimistic mood. Tax revenues were up. Prices were relatively stable and social spending had increased significantly, improving living standards in rural areas, providing assistance for the ill and making life easier for the aged. The economy continued to grow and the average worker had never been so well off.

The Canadian workplace continued to transform itself. Millions of Canadians now depended on American corporations for their incomes, making the national economy more vulnerable than ever to economic downturns originating south of the border. The makeup of the national workforce was changing too, with the proportion of women to men having doubled in the past twenty years.

In keeping with the anti-establishment mood of the young, it was a time of "liberation," a word that encompassed everything from bohemian wardrobes to psychedelic drugs to gay rights to terrorist threats to "the pill." Feminism, environmentalism, even campus Marxism had become trendy, as there was hardly an ism that affluence couldn't afford.

The Liberals were still in power in Ottawa, now under a new prime minister, the dashing and youthful Pierre Elliot Trudeau. Swept into office in 1968 on a euphoric upwelling of Trudeaumania, the elegant bachelor seemed to embody the era, with his easy flouting of convention and glib dismissals of political orthodoxies. The ecstasy proved to be short-lived, however, as the realities of politics and the shifting tides of Canada's contradictory culture caught up to the young philosopher-king and his subjects. Paradox was the order of the day and the glittering surfaces of Canada's soaring office buildings and indoor malls concealed disturbing undercurrents.

Unemployment, nationwide, had fallen to less than 4 percent. The percentage of idle youth, however, hung stubbornly near double that. And by the summer of 1970, the problem of unemployment had become largely a question about what to do with young people. Over half a million students had descended on the labour market and large numbers of "transient youth" were making life difficult for city authorities in many parts of the country. The federal government did its best to ease the situation by turning armouries into "crash pads," but the remedy fed the unease, in Vancouver at least, when a group of young militants occupied the armoury and refused to vacate.

Idle and disaffected young people had already caused disruption during the '60s in Europe and the United States. The federal government had begun looking for ways to channel the energy and exuberance of the country's youth, at the same time helping them develop some of the skills they would need to manage their working lives.

An active manpower policy, once again, was seen as the best possible approach. In the spring of 1970, some seventy-five Canada Manpower Centres for Students were opened across the country, with a primary objective to match youthful workers with employers looking for summer help. Over 130,000 student placements were made the following summer as young Canadians found their way into jobs with the military, the public service and the business community.

Youth Employment Services (YES) opened in 1968 in Toronto as the first youth employment counselling centre in Canada. Shown here are early staff members including Norma Penner (far right) the Executive Director from 1975-1989.

Projections for the summer of 1971 suggested that even greater numbers of young people would be looking for work. Knowing that there were not enough jobs to go around, the federal government decided to expand its youth employment efforts, allocating $58 million to programs for the coming year.

Canada Manpower's Employ-ment Centres for Students were expanded and upgraded, as they would be every summer thereafter. Aware that the centres were likely to handle only a fraction of the need, Ottawa began to cast about for new and different ways to provide employment opportunities for Canadian youth.

The first such initiative, known as Opportunities for Youth (OFY), was announced in March, 1971, by none other than the prime minister himself. "The government believes," Pierre Trudeau said, "that youth is sincere in its efforts to improve society and that young people are anxious to work and to engage in activities which are intended to make Canada a better place in which to live…we intend to challenge them to see if they have the stamina and self-discipline to follow through on their criticism and advice."

Canadian youth were encouraged to propose make-work projects of their own invention. Once approved, these projects were supported by cheques from the federal government and young people across the country went to work on the "clearing of hiking paths, cleaning of river beds and care of the elderly and children."[1]

It paved the way for another program of a similar nature, this one not restricted to youth. In the most interventionist approach it had ever taken to the workplace, the federal government went on to establish Local Initiatives Programs (LIP) for workers of all ages. Over the course of the decade, hundreds of millions of public dollars would be spent on job creation projects of this sort. "Fitting the man to the job" became, in these instances at least, "paying people to do the work they wanted to do."

Programs like LIP and OFY marked the beginning of a massive shift in the ways in which the federal government would be involved in the working lives of Canadians. No longer did government initiatives for the unemployed feature only income replacement and a labour exchange to match jobs and workers. There were funds for job-training programs, mostly through educational institutions, although also on the job. There were programs to teach people how to look for

YOUTH EMPLOYMENT SERVICES

Conceived and born in the summer of 1968—the "summer of love"—the Youth Employment Service (YES) was an idea whose time had clearly come. In cities and towns across the continent, streets and parks were filled with young people; a great wave of post-war babies was (almost) all grown up and many of them had nowhere to go. They might have had flowers in their hair, but Wally Seccombe, a young YMCA youth worker in Toronto, saw that for many of them, living in the streets and parks wasn't about freedom and fun. It was about being unemployed.

"I said to my dad that the biggest thing that most of them needed was a job," Seccombe remembers. "And he just got going on this." His father, the late Wally Seccombe Sr., a successful businessman and member of the Rotary Club, approached the problem with vigour. His fellow Rotarians bought into his vision as soon as he pitched it.

"I still remember those businessmen sitting around our basement," Wally Seccombe recalls. "They set up a committee and they exerted pressure on one another to give young people jobs. Guys just phoned around to other guys in business. The really interesting thing about YES was how it just took off."

YES did take off, but unlike many other innovative ideas of the era, this one stayed aloft. While the Rotarians and their ad hoc committee networked, the late Grant Lowery, an energetic and visionary youth services supervisor at the YMCA, put the organization in place. Very quickly, YES became the template for a distinctive form of storefront employment office, refer-

work and referrals to specialized counsellors for those with severe employment problems.

Far from the mean-spirited workhouse policies of yesteryear, the federal government was running a publicly funded, multi-service organization to support Canadian workers with a broad range of local labour market assistance.

Expanding the partnerships

Yet another initiative to come out of this era of big-spending government was Ottawa's Outreach Program, which, over the years, helped to finance the development and delivery of services provided by   the not-for-profit sector. Encouraged by federal funds, many community agencies and organizations integrated community based training opportunities into the services they offered.

For most of the century, since before Etta St. John Wileman's day in fact, not-for-profit organizations and agencies had relied on volunteers, local fundraising campaigns and philanthropic grants and donations to cover their operating costs. Now, under the banner of its active manpower policy, Ottawa began to earmark funds from programs like Outreach specifically for community-based training and employment initiatives.

The number of Canadian not-for-profit organizations had grown

ral service and vocational guidance and counselling centre aimed specifically at young people. "It became a powerful model," says Seccombe, now a professor of sociology at the University of Toronto. "It was creative, synergistic. It worked." Thirty years later, it would continue to work, recognizing and addressing the unique problems faced by youthful job-seekers. YES was never simply about finding a volume of job vacancies and putting young people into the slots. "They needed counselling too," says Seccombe. "A counsellor who could help them and keep them going."

This tended to work both ways. Employers knew they had access to the counsellors as well and were not simply left with a youthful employee who might have an erratic work history or who might be dealing with social problems. Very often, remembers Wally Seccombe, the results were astonishing. "Lots of these kids had never had a job for longer than three months," he says. "Then once in this, they change their orientation to work. All of a sudden you've got these kids and their lives are changed. Magic is happening."

As the first Canadian youth employment centre, Ontario-based YES served as the model for similar services across the country. Delegations from Britain, Japan, the West Indies, the Netherlands and Australia have observed the YES model and incorporated features of the program into their own youth programs. The remarkable success of this model for intervention and vocational guidance might be best summed up and explained by the final line of the YES mission statement: "The mission of YES is not simply to find a job for the client. It is essentially an effort to assist young people and others to identify their capabilities and assist them to become productive members of society."

considerably over the course of the 20th century, especially since the Second World War. Many had come into existence to assist and advocate on behalf of people with special needs in a variety of geographic, economic and cultural communities. As often as not, these needs included training, employment assistance and some form of career or vocational counselling.

The Trudeau government wanted programs that could respond quickly to the changing needs of people in the workplace, especially those who had trouble adapting and finding work. Community agencies were close to the communities they served and sensitive to the barriers encountered by the employment-disadvantaged. And because not-for-profit organizations could often complement government resources with philanthropic contributions, they were seen as good investments and appropriate partners.

Some of these organizations were large and had a national reach, like the YMCA and YWCA, which had had offices in Canada since the mid-19th century. Others, like Big Brothers and the Canadian National Institute for the Blind, were established in the early decades of the 20th century. During the Great Depression, the John Howard Society was founded in Vancouver to help men as they were released from prison. After the Second World War, branches opened in most other major cities. The Elizabeth Fry Society sprang up in British Columbia and Ontario in the '50s & '60s to help women and girls who were in conflict with the law.

Ottawa's funding of job creation programs was a mixed blessing. On the one hand, it undeniably helped to expand the career related programs and services offered by the not-for-profit sector. Not-for-profit employment programs, dramatically increased the assistance available to those with special needs. It is also true, however, that the restrictions and conditions placed on the grants meant that programs had to be constantly customized to fit the government's shifting objectives and priorities. And because applications for funding had to be made within each fiscal year, it tended to make longer term planning and staffing more difficult. As such, federal funding was not targeted at building an infrastructure of services but rather one-shot short term programs to meet specific needs.

Standing on his shoulders

In the mid-1970s, Gerald Cosgrave retired from the Counselling Foundation of Canada to his apple orchard outside Toronto, although he remained active for some years writing and consulting in the field. Ultimately, Cosgrave added seven publications to the growing body of Canadian-published career and employment resources.

Cosgrave's contributions to the field had been recognized by the Canadian Psychological Association as early as 1972 and, a couple of years later, by Toronto's YMCA Counselling Service, of which he had been Executive Director for twenty years. It was at the YMCA awards ceremony that Cosgrave met Bill O'Byrne, a young graduate in clinical psychology from the University of Ottawa who had recently joined the YMCA Counselling Service. He became both a friend and a mentor,

O'Byrne recalls, and eventually Cosgrave asked O'Byrne to revise a couple of his books.

O'Byrne was honoured by the request. "If there is one person in this country who turned career counselling into a respected entity," he says, "it was Gerald Cosgrave. He was a humble man, he was very Canadian in that way. But I think he was powerfully influential. It was Cosgrave who made the difference. He did it by doing the work. People came back or they told their friends and then they started telling their kids. Gerald Cosgrave is the person I am standing on the shoulders of," says Bill O'Byrne, with a note of both respect and quiet pride. "I'm picking up his torch."

In 1984, Frank Lawson died and his son, Donald, assumed the chairmanship of the Foundation and established an active board of directors to govern it. "We took over a foundation that been a private giving fund of father's," recalls Donald Lawson. "We had about $1.5 million per year to give away wisely. And the first thing the board had to do was set its own goals and objectives and then find some projects that fit within those."

Elizabeth McTavish

Elizabeth McTavish, who had been with the Foundation since 1970 to assist Gerald Cosgrave, was named Counselling Director when Gerald Cosgrave retired. McTavish, at the time, defined the role of the Foundation's Board of Directors as the "provision of grants designed to improve the quality and quantity of counselling." Until the mid-1990s, the university sector was to remain the primary recipient of grants from The Counselling Foundation of Canada. The most intense involvement was at York University where McTavish also functioned as director of the university's Career Counselling Centre which the CFC had helped implement and had supported for many years.

Foundation funding was also targeted at campus student services. Demand for counselling, career and placement-related guidance had grown throughout the 1980s. As governments retrenched, Canada Employment Centres on university campuses had been closed. While this had little impact on the handful of Canadian universities, including the University of Toronto which had developed its own career-related student services, other post-secondary institutions had to scramble to replace the centres.

During this period, more than twenty Canadian universities would receive multi-year funding from The Counselling Foundation of Canada to establish or enhance on-campus career services for students. This was a critical time on university campuses as universities for the first time had to decide whether they would internally fund career and placement centres. Transitional funding from the federal government was provided as a negotiated arrangement between universities and the federal government. Federal funding for on-campus services was not to last, though, making the quest of career counselling to be seen as having a legitimate place within a university community all the more challenging.

Oil shock, "stagflation" and a shift in economic wisdom

In the mid-1970s, in a sobering demonstration of the growing economic power of Professor McLuhan's global village, the Trudeau government's big spending policies ran smack into a wall of brand new realities.

Too unpopular to finance through taxes, the Vietnam War was paid for by an expanded money supply. The resulting inflationary crisis prompted the American government to cut spending and tighten credit, with the result that unemployment figures in the United States began to climb. Washington responded by imposing trade restrictions and the impact was quickly felt north of the border.

At the end of 1973, an oil crisis in the Middle East added to the havoc already plaguing economies throughout the western world, sending prices soaring at the gas pumps in Canada as well. The dreaded vortex of inflation came spiralling not far behind.

At the same time, the numbers of Canada's unemployed also began to climb. The combination of higher prices and fewer jobs was a new phenomenon, or at least one not seen in the thirty years since the end of the war, for which the new name "stagflation" was coined.

In 1975, with inflation raging over 10 percent, the Governor of the Bank of Canada announced a return to "tight money" policies as the only way to control inflation and achieve economic growth.

The days of deep-pocket government intervention were numbered, it seemed. Accepting the new economic wisdom, the Trudeau government imposed wage and price controls within the year, signalling a shift away from its preoccupation with the unemployed and focusing instead on price stability. Over the next several years, inflation did come down. So, however, did the productive output of the country. Failing to recognize the confusion in its policies, Ottawa continued to spend, driving its own balance sheet into the red. At the same time, unemployment climbed to over 8 percent, making the need for a variety of assistance programs more obvious, among them some form of career and employment assistance.

For much of the century, however compelling the need in which it was rooted and however dedicated the efforts of the professionals driving its evolution, the field of career councselling grew in relative obscurity, unrecognized beyond the specialized sectors of the economy in which it was being nurtured. To those fortunate enough to receive its attentions, it was a resource of considerable value. To society at large, however, the field of career counselling had next to no identity.

It is a matter of debate just when the branching shape of the field first became visible. There are many possibilities as there are particular points of view. Whatever the defining moment, it clearly happened in the post industrial era, when the widespread need for some form of individualized assistance for Canadian workers and Canadian students became impossible to ignore, and governments began to respond.

[1] John Hunter, *The Employment Challenge* (Ottawa: Government of Canada).

CREATING A
National Identity
OF
Career
Counsellors

In the 1970s, reflecting the country's regional diversity, the often contentious relationship between Ottawa and the provinces and the various degrees of commitment by individual provinces to career development, different approaches and infrastructure began appearing in different parts of the country.

Increasingly, career counsellors were able to offer their clients opportunities for hands-on exposure to possible career choices through programs such as cooperative education programs, which became increasingly popular at the secondary and post-secondary levels in the 1970s and 1980s. Co-ops were the result of the productive marriage of two consequent needs: students uninterested or less inclined to be confined to traditional forms of learning in favour of learning by doing; and a growing awareness on the part of employers that providing co-op placements was an effective way of identifying potential full-time employees. Along similar lines were apprenticeship programs, offered primarily through trade unions where the tradition of the guild system had carried on at least in this way of introducing younger trainees to the trade.

A local Youth Employment Services program created in response to the special needs of young people in Toronto blossomed with the help of federal and provincial funding. Provincial funding nurtured the development of an Ontario wide network of Youth Employment Counselling Centres. These centres quickly became community focal points during the 70s and 80s when youth employment reached all time double digit highs. It was in fact these community based centres that were able to reach out-of-school youth, who had become, with the social trends of these decades, increasingly marginalized from society.

Much innovation in the field emanated from this network of youth centres, which was found to be applicable to youth in schools, as well as school-leavers. Similar types of youth-focused centres formed across the country—in Alberta, for instance, Career Centres were developed by the Alberta Department of Career Development. Governments worked in partnership with these non-profit centres and recognized their unique ability to respond quickly and adapt to young people's changing employment counselling needs. It is these early partnership arrangements that paved the way for the eventual development of joint initiatives between governments, labour and community organizations in all sorts of other fields including health care and cultural development.

Primary resource industries, like oil extraction, were the mainstay of the western economy in Canada late into the twentieth century

© John de Visser/Masterfile

New directions in the oil patch

Playing a theme politically popular in the west, Alberta's new premier, Peter Lougheed, accused the federal government of pursuing policies that supported growth in central Canada at the expense of provincial development strategies. After thirty-six years of Social Credit rule, Lougheed had won an upset victory in 1971 by promising to establish policies to develop and diversify Alberta's economy. Part of the plan was the development of an active manpower policy.

The oil patch was booming. The very crisis that would soon hold the rest of the country to high interest rate ransom had fuelled unprecedented growth in Canada's major oil producing province. The oil sands north of Edmonton in Fort McMurray and Cold Lake were being developed. Across the province, exploration crews and drilling rigs were working at full capacity. And in both Edmonton and Calgary, construction cranes dotted the cityscape.

Severe shortages of skilled workers hampered industry's ability to keep pace with the boom however, and the province's employers were complaining. More and better training was needed to provide workers with the right skills for the work that needed to be done. At the same time, the demographics were worrisome, according to Dave Chabillon, who became the Deputy Minister of Field Services for the province's labour ministry, called Alberta Advanced Education and Career Development. He felt many of the province's skilled workers were nearing retirement age and no provisions had been made to replace them.

The notion of career development was barely understood at the time, even within government circles. "I had one of my bosses ask me, 'What is this career development? Is it a personnel shop for the government?'" Chabillion recalls. He responded, "Personnel shops take care of selection, recruitment and placement. A labour market ministry has a lot more on its plate.

"You need to do a fair amount of analytical work in the sense of demographics associated with the labour market. You need to look at those people who, in fact, are outside the labour market looking in and wanting in. The indigenous people, women, handicapped, visible minorities. The federal government didn't even count aboriginal people into their labour force statistics. But they're Albertans, they're Canadians, they have to be folded into the labour market."

Alberta Career Centres were opened throughout the province, becoming local repositories for training and employment information and career counselling. A Career Resources division was established to produce relevant labour market information and career planning and job search materials for the range of clients that passed through the Centres' doors.

Adults, unemployed or not, could access career information and advice. Employers could find information about government training initiatives and employment programs. And Alberta's educators could gather current data and find career planning information for their students, to help them make solid career decisions.

Among those specifically targeted were teachers, says Chabillion, a provincial park warden turned public servant. "There was a need for educational institutions to start thinking in terms of the labour market," he says. "The attitude of a lot of educators at that time, and I hope it has changed, was if you give an individual a broad educational background, they'll be well set to move into whatever walk of life they choose. A lot of the training and education people were receiving in post secondary education wasn't labour market oriented."

Nor were high-school guidance teachers and counsellors helping students gain a broad perspective of their options, says Barry Day, who was recruited in 1979 out of the educational system and who became Director of the Career Resources branch in Alberta.

Day is one of many people who entered the field from a background in guidance counselling. He "fell into it," as he puts it, in Moose Jaw, Saskatchewan in the '60s when he taught physical education and coached the school's athletic teams.

Although he enjoyed teaching and coaching, it was the guidance counselling that really "lit me up," Day recalls, the enthusiasm still evident more than thirty years later. "Most of the kids we had in the technical stream had failed at least once before they got to us. And it was our job to find a way to help them build a foundation for the future.

"One of the things we did was convince business students to take a technical class and technical students to take a business class," he recalls. "They got a better perspective. So it broadened their horizons rather than narrowed them. And that's what made sense from a career development perspective. We didn't call it career development at the time. We simply called it teaching kids, or influencing kids to learn through a variety of ways."

Day had moved to the Edmonton area in the mid-1970s to become

---

From self-help to support groups
In 1973, psychologist Nathan Azrin started job clubs in the United States. These didn't start formally in Canada until 1982, when the Employment Support Services Branch of the CEIC conducted a pilot study at the Peterborough Youth Employment Centre in Ontario. Within three weeks, 90 percent of the participants found employment and clubs were set up at sixty centres across Canada. Groups of ten to twelve job seekers, under the supervision of trained employment counsellors, met every day for about four hours until jobs were obtained. The strategy was to create an intensive and structured learning experience, using the techniques of behaviourism such as positive reinforcement, multiple reinforcers, behavioural contracting and other procedures. The idea was for participants to learn how to conduct a job search by performing all the elements of job-seeking in a controlled environment.

assistant superintendent of a county school district. At the time, guidance in most high schools tended to be "test and tell them" supplemented with academic planning for university bound studies.

Teachers and students alike needed a broader perspective on career development, Day says. And the exciting part of his new job as Director of the province's Career Resources branch would be coming up with products and materials to provide just that.

Innovation in Quebec

Throughout the country, in the years to come, there would be many stories like those of Dave Chabillon and Barry Day, as career counselling principles and techniques developed in one context were reworked and combined to fill the requirements of another. The commitment and vision of the field's pioneers had given rise to something of practical value and the more pressing and varied the need, the greater the potential for response.

Canada's geographic and cultural diversity exercised an enormous influence on the nature of work and the requirements of the workplace. The potential variations for effective career counselling were virtually limitless. Every job was different, as was every job applicant. The challenge of fitting the one to the other would create a complex, multi-branched industry before the century was out.

Nowhere, perhaps, were the challenges more pronounced than in the province of Quebec. And nowhere was the provincial government more likely to resist intervention by its counterpart in Ottawa.

Language and culture are of supreme importance to the people of North America's only formally constituted French-speaking region. It is not surprising, therefore, that the career counselling industry which took root in that province was not so much a branch of something begun elsewhere as it was an entirely different organism.

Quebec's educational system prior to the 1960s was a complicated mix of insular subsystems, organized along denominational and linguistic fault lines. They all functioned to provide education to Quebec's youth but without a common purpose or mandate. Vocational guidance had been available to some students in some private schools in the province as early as the 1930s. In Quebec's public school system, some counselling services had been offered since the 1940s. But counsellors' duties were poorly defined and those asked to fulfill them were often mistrusted by other school employees.

Not until secular educational reform began redesigning Quebec's school system did the profession gain a firm foothold in the province's education system. The election of Liberal Premier Jean Lesage in 1960 had heralded a time of dramatic change, the so-called "Quiet

Société GRICS

As a private, not-for-profit corporation, Société GRICS has been meeting the information technology needs of Quebec school boards since 1985. The vast majority of school boards enjoy many diversified GRICS products and services for administrative management, school management, telecommunication and, of course, those services most directly related to career and educational needs – BIM, la banque d'instruments de mesure (a database of questions and exams) and REPÈRES (a computerized databank of educational and vocational services).

Francophone Canadian educational planning counsellors, employment counsellors and career development practioners continue to have access to relevant and up-to-date resources through Société GRICS.

Revolution." A Royal Commission of Inquiry on Education was established and Alphonse Parent, the Vice Rector of Laval University, was appointed chair. The Parent Committee's report, released in 1964, articulated a need to "restructure the province's educational facilities to meet the needs of modern society with its increased pluralism and greater concentration in urban and industrial centres."

And restructure they did. A provincial Ministry of Education was established. The Minister of Youth, Paul Gerin-Lajoie, was named the province's first Minister of Education since 1875. Comprehensive reform moved through the province's educational system at an incredible rate. Within a matter of a few years, a highly centralized, lay-controlled system of secondary schools and a network of junior colleges had been established. The response from the population was equally astonishing. Between 1960 and 1970 alone, enrollment in the province's secondary schools more than doubled. College enrollments increased by 82 percent in the same time frame and university enrollments by 162 percent.

State intervention in education had also had a positive impact on the position of guidance counsellors in Quebec's schools. During the '60s and '70s the government institutionalized the counsellors' professional activity. And the educational theory of vocational guidance strongly influenced the practice of career guidance in the schools.

By the 1970s, career counselling in the province was professionally designated and regulated: In order to work as a career counsellor in the province's schools or other settings, a candidate was required to be a member of either the Corporation of Counsellors or the Corporation of Psychologists. Post-graduate studies to at least a master's level were essential in both cases. Most educational programs in psychology in Quebec's universities included some consideration of guidance as required instruction. At Laval University, the program was especially designed and organized for counsellors.

A key goal of the Quiet Revolution was "rattrapage," a concerted effort to bring Quebec's economic standards in line with the rest of North America and to bring francophone incomes in line with anglophone incomes. Economic parity was one thing, a learned respect for language and culture was another. In both instances, professional guidance for students was seen as essential. As programs were developed to meet the province's unique set of needs, Quebec set a standard unparalleled and unrecognized by most of the country at the time.

Gerald Cosgrave, as the Director of The Counselling Foundation of Canada, once asked Aurele Gagnon, the Director of Guidance in the Quebec Department of Education, why the state of the counselling field in Quebec had become so advanced. Gagnon attributed its evolved state to differences in attitudes and outlook between the French and the English.

"English Canadians tend to be very practical," Cosgrave recalled Gagnon explaining. "When they recognize a need, they are eager to do something about it right away, even if it is only a matter of giving would-be counsellors a few summer courses. The French are more philosophical and rational. When it is decided that guidance is needed, they tend to think of the full implications and decide what knowledge and skills a counsellor should have. They feel it is better not to do the job at all, than to do it with less than the required knowledge and skills."

Long term planning of this kind was complemented by Quebec's single-minded efforts to control, as much as possible, the province's educational, training and employment services. For example, the Parti Quebecois government, elected in 1976, established a number of manpower offices that provided essentially the same services as Canada Manpower. The PQ tried but failed to dislodge the federal government from playing a role in manpower training in the province. This determination to become masters in its own career development house would become ever more pronounced in the years ahead.

The federal government as referral agent and worker provider

At the beginning of the '70s, Canadian industrial incomes ranked second highest in the world. Nine years later, they had fallen to seventh place. Average individual purchasing power had shrunk significantly, but still economists wanted wages squeezed more. Tight money policies continued, and the combination of high interest rates and spending cuts virtually guaranteed continued unemployment.

Labour market officials now had an astonishing range of tools available to them with which to intervene in the labour market but there was

CO-OPERATIVE EDUCATION

Russian cosmonauts headed into space, trailing clouds of technological glory and the countries left on the ground wondered if they had missed the boat or, in this case, the satellite. Technology, engineering and scientific expertise were much on the minds of the populations of Canada and the U.S. as universities and schools scrambled to catch up to Russia's perceived scientific superiority.

It was the button-down 1950s, but a group of Ontario businessmen had a bold idea for ratcheting up Canada's technological and scientific acumen: A technology-oriented university, the centrepiece of which would be an engineering program based on the concept of co-operative education.

Thus, co-op education, an idea that had taken firm root in the U.S. at the University of Cincinnati some fifty years earlier, finally found fertile ground in Canada.

Waterloo College, which would go on to become the University of Waterloo, was expanding in the 1950s and in the newly founded faculty of science the seed was planted. Pragmatic business people like the founders of Waterloo's early program may have thought the alliance between the eventual employers of students and their educators was natural and fitting, but there were early detractors. According to Bruce McCallum and James Wilson, authors of *They Said It Wouldn't Work - A History of Cooperative Education in Canada*, "Waterloo was visited by representatives from other institutions who only wanted to criticize the process."

Academic purists predicted that the co-op education idea would dilute education, damage the educational procedure and, at any rate, would not be supported by the business community. History would prove them wrong.

no coherent strategy in place as to when, where, how or why they should be applied. Critics pointed to areas of overlap and duplication between programs and worried that clients with special needs could still fall through the cracks.

The federal government role appeared to have been reduced to a modus operandi of quick referrals and quick placements.

During the 1970s, world oil prices tripled and stagflation became the bane of governments throughout the industrialized world. In heightened concerns about the economy, an increasingly conservative mood settled over the smoky inner chambers of ministers and corporate presidents alike. Monetarists argued that keeping interest rates high would shrink the money supply, which had been inflated by excessive credit. "Supply-siders" insisted that lowering taxes for the wealthy would act as an incentive for greater investment in the economy.

Both sides agreed that money spent by governments was unproductive. Government intervention was responsible, the thinking went, for many of the malfunctions in western economies.

By 1978, Ottawa's comfortable budgetary surpluses had metamorphosed to an annual deficit of nearly $12 billion. That same year, after attending a summit of western industrial leaders, Prime Minister Trudeau read the writing on the wall, returned home and disbanded the Anti Inflation Board, cutting taxes, spending and programs.

The decades of federal government investment in the labour market had laid the groundwork for the career counselling and development

During the 1970s, government helped to further the reputation of co-op education by making money available to both secondary and post-secondary institutions keen to explore the benefits of this education model.

By the end of the century, thousands of companies nationwide would employ nearly 68,000 co-op education students. Many of these organizations would make co-op students their preferred choice for permanent hire. And nearly 60 percent of co-op students would continue to work with their placement employer after graduation.

Fundamental to the success of co-operative education was the founding in 1973 of the Canadian Association for Co-operative Education (CAFCE). Firmly established by 1977, CAFCE redefined its mandate and invited employers to become members. By the end of the century, combining the efforts of more than four hundred educators, employers and government officials, the national organization would become one of the world's most widely developed co-op education models.

With post-secondary cooperative education programs ultimately available in fields from arts administration to international development and the recognition by many secondary schools of the value of early "real world" experience, the demand for and appreciation of the concept would continue to expand.

Launched at mid-century with the express purpose of boosting the country's technological abilities, cooperative education would, by the century's close, prove to be a remarkably down-to-earth way of melding academic education and hands-on experience; preparing a new workforce with not just knowledge, but with skills.

field and, although Ottawa would continue to play a significant leading role, cost-cutting was on the way.

The impact of public spending cuts affected every sector. Union policies began to change as well. In the industrial sector in particular, growing numbers of union members were losing jobs with little chance of recall. Concerns about foreign ownership and the branch plant economy sparked demands for a Canadian industrial strategy. Externally controlled, multi-national corporations made employer/employee relations more remote, while central management from afar was seen to facilitate arbitrary shutdowns and layoffs.

Labour increasingly Made-in-Canada

The growth of the self-help movement
During the sixties and seventies a number of books appeared and remained on the best seller lists, which provided advice to job seekers and insight about the career development process. Reflecting the shift from matching a person to the job, to providing the job seeker with more personal choice, mass-market books encouraged individuals to target a desired job and acquire more job-search skills. By far the most popular of these was Richard Bolles' *What Color if Your Parachute*, first commercially published in 1972 and still updated annually.

Since the earliest days of the century, the central Canadian trade union movement had been dominated by American-based unions. Beginning in the mid-1970s, however, that had started to change, as "breakaways" began to form national unions.

In search of new members, union organizers had shifted their focus to Canada's growing service industry, in particular to workers in the public sector. A national postal strike in 1965 had captured the attention of civil servants across the country. With salaries lagging a couple of years behind the private sector, government workers recognized considerable value in collective bargaining rights. By the end of the 1960s, most public sector employees across Canada had been unionized.

Labour policies were also influenced by the growing numbers of women on union membership rolls. For most of the century, the labour movement had largely ignored the needs of female workers, frequently among the most exploited members of the workforce. In the changing workplace of the '70s, women were heavily concentrated on the lower rungs of the public service and, as the organization of the expanding government sector continued, the majority of new "brothers" were sisters.

Higher levels of education were also having an impact. A technologically more sophisticated workplace required better-educated workers who in turn were better informed about their rights. The '60s and '70s had been stormy years on labour fronts, as union negotiators pressed demands for a bigger slice of the economic pie.

"It's completely impossible to give these young people the old hogwash," said a "veteran union man" quoted in *Saturday Night* magazine. "They know too much. For years the companies have been using the educational system as a filter, to save them doing their own thinking about personnel. And now the results are coming in. Now they've got young people working for them who are better educated than the boss."[1]

For the most part, such changes notwithstanding, unions had continued to represent their new members in much the same way as they had their core group in manufacturing, focusing on collective wages, security and working conditions. Generally, throughout Canada's labour history, the career and working-life needs of individual members had been given little consideration. Nor had there been union-sponsored counselling programs or training initiatives to help union members enhance their working skills and potential.

A changing workplace

Labour was by no means oblivious to the changing skill needs of individual workers. As early as the 1930s, labour made some provision for literacy training for members in need of it. In their gathering awareness of their members' needs for "a more satisfying work experience" unions were also being pushed, along with the rest of society, toward "a more elevated conception of the human potential."[2] In the 1970s, the Canadian Labour Congress' Labour College was established in Regina, Saskatchewan. And some unions, notably the Canadian branch of the United Auto Workers, provided university scholarships to some members and their families.

In 1973, in the automotive hub of Windsor, Ontario, the first Union Counsellor Program was developed. Volunteers were trained to provide union members with assistance to help them define their own needs and to refer them onward to other services available in the community.

Help of this kind soon became necessary, not just in specific pockets but throughout the Canadian workplace, as unemployment figures continued to inch upwards. Some union leaders began to push for centres that would help members who had lost their jobs or were temporarily laid off. By 1977, also in Windsor, the first union-run Unemployed Help Centre was up and running. Within a year, another was established in Toronto.

Commencing in the 1960s, employers had begun to pay more attention to fair and equitable treatment of their employees, in large part because of the growing body of labour law. Provincial employment standards legislation had been established, and human rights and occupational health and safety laws implemented. Gradually, a full range of employer obligations and responsibilities would be legislated, including minimum wages, hours of work, overtime, daily and weekly rest times, statutory holidays, vacations and vacation pay, maternity leave and even time off to vote.

Career transition services, including career assessment and job search counselling, were made available, though at first only to a small, elite management group. For a few valued employees, career counselling was also made available. Demographic projections for the corporate workforce had begun to predict a decline in the supply of senior managers. Some major employers, looking for a strategy to ensure their supply of competent executives, established internal career management programs, reminiscent of the career counselling provided employees of large organizations like Canadian General Electric in the 1950s.

Counselling of this kind became a management perk in a few public and private sector organizations during the '70s. Often it was part of employer-sponsored management training initiatives.

National Consultation on Career Development (NATCON)

Founded in 1975, the National Consultation on Career Development, or NATCON, as it is widely known, is held each January in Ottawa's Conference Centre. It is the country's most comprehensive professional development opportunity for career counselling practitioners. Bringing together counselling professionals from diverse environments—secondary schools, training colleges, universities, outplacement services, all levels of government and employee assistance providers—NATCON provides a forum for state-of-the-art information on career counselling and placement in Canada and around the world.

Kathie Swenson, a Nova Scotia guidance counsellor turned provincial government bureaucrat, attended the first NATCON conference and almost every one thereafter, until she retired in the early '90s. "They were tremendously valuable," she recalled. "The support of the federal government enabled people across the country to come together who never in the world would have known each other otherwise. To come together and exchange ideas and information. I wouldn't have known what was going on in Alberta, or elsewhere in the country. It meant that we all didn't have to reinvent the wheel, that we could build on each other's work."

According to Stuart Conger, who initiated the first conference, building on each other's work was what NATCON was all about. "It was really a campaign to try to bring people together, to give them ideas, information and resources." Twenty people attended in 1975.

Until 1985, NATCON was sponsored exclusively by the federal department of Employment and Immigration Canada. However, the mood of fiscal restraint that gripped Mulroney's Conservative government in the '80s soon reached even into this specialized corner, and for a time the national gathering was threatened by budgetary cutbacks. In 1987, NATCON became the responsibility of a partnership of The Counselling Foundation of Canada, HRDC and the University of Toronto Career Centre. The Counselling Foundation of Canada was to provide the funding; HRDC, the facilities, translation equipment and interpretation personnel; and the University of Toronto Career Centre, the organization, administration and program.

Under the new partnership, NATCON became the largest bilingual conference in the world. Delegates came from all sectors delivering career development. The number of sessions expanded to include over 150 per conference with over 200 presenters. NATCON began attracting delegates from the United States, Asia, Australia and Europe. Participants numbered over 1200 in 2000.

NATCON has played a fundamental role in providing a national forum for sharing and disseminating information on emerging trends, cutting edge practices, and state-of-the-art theories and approaches.

---

[1] "Labour Lays it on the Line" by Mungo James, *Saturday Night*, December 1966.
[2] Steven Langdon, "Review of Industrial Democracy & Canadian Labour" in *Canadian Forum*, September 197

TECHNOLOGICAL
Advance,
Restructuring
AND THE
TRAINING OF A
Profession

"Whenever we face international competition," the chairman of the Science Council of Canada said, "we have no choice but to be as productive as possible, including using all of the new technologies, even if this means putting people out on the street." He might have been offering a historical perspective on the management paradigm that swept through the world of big business in the 1980s, had he not been speaking on the eve of its appearance. Stuart Smith was simply speaking the practical truth, from a particular point of view. Suddenly, it seemed, pulling into focus like the image in a camera's lens, the reality of a global market had appeared. It had been gathering strength for a decade and more, in the expansion of the communications infrastructure, the proliferation of so-called "multi-national" corporations and the increasingly rapid movement of money around the world.

The other major workplace trend of the era was a rapidly growing small business sector. While large corporations downsized, disgorging people into the streets, small businesses were opening up in record numbers, many started by those orphaned by big business. Two distinct, interrelated trends emerged: a greater dependency on technology; and the rise of the small business sector.

Technology was becoming ever more sophisticated and, with each new generation of computers, workplaces throughout the entire world were changing, in service of greater efficiency and a sharper competitive edge. Throughout the global marketplace, capital was stretching its horizons. Japan was on the rise and, hard on its heels, were the "Four Tigers" of Singapore, Taiwan, South Korea and Hong Kong. The vanquished foe of the Second World War had emerged in a very different guise. The east-west contest had shifted to the cash register and the competition was proving to be stiff.

It was a serious wakeup call throughout the west. Competition was no longer confined to corporate backyards. The global village was a marketplace and corporate competition happened everywhere, even continents away. Another round of "oil shock" late in the 1970s had sent inflation spiking upward again in the United States and, by the time the monetarist hammer had pounded it back down again, the economy was in deep recession.

"Lean and mean" became the management mantra of the day. "Restructuring" and "re-engineering" were the lead items on large corporate agendas everywhere. Threatened by the prowess of their new competitors and experiencing the spiraling costs of energy and labour in their domestic economies, western mega-corporations reinvented themselves. They introduced new, labour-saving technology or moved production offshore to locate in more cost-effective sites around the world where labour was abundant and cheap, taxes were lower and there were fewer environmental regulations. The cost in the wreckage they left behind would be measured in terms of jobs.

Prime Minister Brian Mulroney, with German Chancellor Helmut Kohl, U.S. President Ronald Reagan, and Britain's Prime Minister Thatcher, at a meeting of the Heads of State of the G7 countries, in 1988.

CP Picture Archive (Fred Chartrand)

Both Ronald Reagan and Margaret Thatcher had an abiding faith in markets as self-correcting; they rejected pump priming as the way to keep unemployment from rising. Eventually, Reagan's "military Keynsianism" of vastly increasing military expenditures would serve much the same purpose. From 1981 to 1983, a new financial orthodoxy was emerging.

In Canada, it was only a matter of time. In 1981, interest rates hit a post-war high of 22.5 percent. Stung by the cost of credit, consumers stopped shopping. The combination was too much. The economy took a nosedive. Mass layoffs, shutdowns and bankruptcies followed. The country's gross national product fell by four full percentage points in 1982 alone, the first drop of such magnitude since the Dirty Thirties. The workplace was in turmoil.

Staggered by the growing dimensions of the need, the federal government was hard-pressed to keep up. Increased demands on programs such as unemployment insurance, social assistance and employment creation forced spending ever higher. And the deficit continued to grow.

It was by far the worst economic downturn since the Great Depression, notwithstanding the fact that the decade had started out in a mood of relative prosperity. In the rarefied air around Parliament Hill, events had been even livelier than usual. Pierre Trudeau was back in the Prime Minister's Office, despite having lost the '79 election to Joe Clark and "resigned from political life" altogether—all in the space of less than a year.

Power had not worn well for Clark. Oil prices, interest rates and increasing concern over an impending referendum on sovereignty in Quebec had proved a thorny mix for the rookie prime minister. A tough budget that attempted to appease Alberta's oil patch at the expense of central Canada had sounded the death knell for his government.

Defeated in the Commons, the Tories had been forced to return to the polls. Even then, they might have had some hope of carrying the country, had it not been for Trudeau's unexpected resumption of the Liberal leadership. In February 1980, the enigmatic Trudeau had achieved his third majority government. "Welcome to the 1980s," he greeted his jubilant supporters. Welcome indeed to one of the most difficult, chaotic and adversarial times to govern in the history of the nation, he might well have said, had he known what the balance of the decade held in store.

Within a year the economy had begun its downward spiral, although it appeared to go all but unnoticed in Ottawa, where the prime minister remained preoccupied with issues of national unity, the constitution and Quebec.

A provincial referendum had failed to achieve a mandate for the Parti Quebecois' dream of "sovereignty association." "Non" had been the response of 60 percent of the electorate to the proposal for negotiations with Ottawa. It was a victory for federalism and Trudeau had moved quickly forward with his attempts at constitutional reform, turning patriation into a "personal crusade" and ultimately achieving it, although at the incalculable cost of fractured national unity.

"The British North America Act was dead," observed historian Desmond Morton. "On April 17, 1982, the Queen proclaimed the Constitution Act. At the cold, rainy Ottawa ceremony, Quebec was not represented."[1]

The struggle for a national policy

By the early 1980s, the former Canada Manpower had been replaced by the Canada Employment and Immigration Commission (CEIC). It was a huge bureaucracy with a sweeping network of local centres managed actively by headquarters in Ottawa. Political and public service authorities were "so busy struggling to cope," according to employment service historian John Hunter, "that they didn't have time for long-term planning."

In the 1980 Speech from the Throne, the Liberal government had announced that new economic policies would be required "to provide jobs, promote growth, improve regional balance and offer a fair distribution of economic opportunity." Active labour market policies were critical to its national development strategy, the government proclaimed, and it was committed to using them to improve the employment picture across the country.[3]

"Attempts to develop a new conceptual framework for employment policies and programs...had to be done 'on the fly.'" There was no overarching vision of government's objectives in the workplace, in other words, and "many of the labour market tools had been developed in response to ad hoc situations and were not part of any coherent, overall labour market strategy."[2]

The National Training Act and the need for labour market information

Following two task forces, which were commissioned to address employment and job creation, the federal government zeroed in on occupational training as important. The government's response to the challenge, at least in part, was found in the National Training Act of 1982, which called for greater cooperation between the provinces and the federal government regarding the training of Canadian workers. The act introduced the concept of "national demand occupations" and included greater support for the training of high level skills.

In addition to introducing a Skills Growth Fund to offer provinces support for the expansion and updating of training facilities, the act also opened the door to the country's not-for-profit, community-based training organizations, allowing them to submit proposals for funding.

At the same time, labour market forecasting became part of federal government policy. A labour market intelligence system, dubbed the Canadian Occupational Projection System (COPS), was introduced to predict future occupational supply and demand nationwide, and to make that information available to workers, students, employers and to employment and career counsellors.

As Canada's industrial and natural resource sectors continued to restructure under the combined pressures of changing technology and heightened competition, the need for cooperative ventures to address Canada's workforce and training needs was growing. In 1983, the government attempted to institutionalize cooperation on labour market issues and established the Canadian Labour Market and Productivity Centre (CLMPC).

Charged with conducting analysis and making recommendations regarding some of the employment and skills issues confronting Canadian workers, the centre brought people together from business, labour and government to look for ways to improve Canada's competitiveness and economic growth. Forging cooperative, cross-sectoral partnerships was no easy undertaking, however. "As is common with new organizations," reports John Hunter, "the centre spent much of its first few years reconciling differing perceptions and expectations."

"Business, labour and government representatives each had their own ideas about the proper goals and functioning of the centre," he goes on. "A consensus eventually emerged however, and the Canadian Labour Market and Productivity Centre became part of Canada's labour market infrastructure."

The CLMPC established task forces to examine "key aspects of federal training programs." These task forces worked independently of government and studied the needs of older workers, of people receiving Unemployment Insurance Benefits, of apprentices and those in cooperative education programs as well as initiatives for people entering the field and those in human resource planning.

Counselling persons with special needs

The Canadian National Institute for the Blind (CNIB) was established in 1918 and for decades has offered a variety of counselling services, including employment counselling, with an initial focus on veterans who were blinded during the war. They branched off into job placement as early as 1920.

Although realizing only limited success initially, by 1928 CNIB was regularly offering both employment counselling and job placement. Most of the services were offered by war-blinded individuals able to help others based on their own experience. There was some assistance in choosing a career, although the scope of occupations offered was fairly limited at first—musician, piano tuner, telephone operator, chair caner, radio technician and concession stand operator. Although we now think of these as stereotypical jobs for individuals who are blind, this was a huge step at the time. Society expected blind people to accept charity, but one of the key roles of the CNIB was to help them find ways to be independent, which often involved employment. The analysis of traditional skills and abilities, as well as creative talents, was a step towards that goal. One of Canada's first dictaphone transcribers (1932) was blind, as were some of the earliest computer programmers.

According to Alex Westgate, Manager, National Employment Services, the CNIB also became a major trainer and employer of persons who are blind, visually impaired or deaf-blind, through its manufacturing and packaging industries. These varied from fully competitive broom and brush manufacturing to smaller operations such as weaving and upholstery to sheltered warehouse packaging services. The jobs available spanned the entire business, from production to sales and marketing, accounting, clerical, purchasing, human resources, maintenance, etc.

In 1968, the first national vocational guidance centre for individuals who were blind or visually impaired was opened in Toronto. People came from all across Canada for vocational testing and assessment. Clerical and telephone operator training courses were also available, as were positions in the broom factory or packaging firm.

Surveys were taken each year of people registered with the CNIB to determine what kinds of education and employment people were finding. Successfully placed people were interviewed and occupational information was collated. Informal peer mentoring was encouraged. As global competition threatened the viability of the manufacturing and packaging operations created by the CNIB, so counsellors placed less emphasis on manual occupations.

Much of this was recorded on tape or braille, as the majority of career counsellors were themselves blind or visually impaired. It was only in the 1980s that the CNIB's guidance centre first sought counsellors with formal training in assessment and counselling. The in-house training systems also expanded to more computer and business applications, as well as ESL (English as a Second Language) for blind newcomers to Canada. Technology made it possible for a myriad of job accommodations to be developed, opening options that had never been considered by the majority of blind or visually impaired people.

Joan Westland, the Executive Director of The Canadian Council on Rehabilitation and Work, describes the evolution of society's treatment of persons with disabilities, as it applies to work: "Employment or vocational counselling really grew out of the sheltered workshop and special training programs of the 1950s and 1960s and were designed around the disability rather than the individual's interests or abilities. Today, we have a bit of a mixed bag. Some counsellors are comfortable providing information and support to people with disabilities, others are not. There are still segregated services (for example, Canadian Hearing Society for the Deaf or CNIB for those who blind). But it would depend on the type of counselling that the person is seeking to determine which service is most appropriate. Years ago, it did not matter what the individual's needs were, they were simply sent to the institution or centre that dealt with disabilities.

Assessment sessions, dexterity and logic tests that could be done manually without the use of text were developed for visually impaired persons. (c. 1985)

"The 'warehouse' period reflects the time up until the 50's and 60's where people with disabilities (known then as cripples and invalids) were kept in large institutions, outside of city centres. They were kept away from the rest of the population. There was little attention paid to individual needs...basic human needs of food, water, air and shelter were provided in various degrees, depending on who was in charge.

"The 'greenhouse' period follows the 'warehouse' period as the institutions started to refine their approach to dealing with people with disabilities. Diagnostic processes are improved so that the classification of people is more complex. In the earlier days, for example, people with Cerebral Palsy, people who were Deaf, had Muscular Dystrophy etc., were all diagnosed as mentally retarded. During the greenhouse period, professionals began to understand that disability was more complex than simply determining that you were different from everyone else. Individual skills, abilities and interests were encouraged to some extent. People were brought out of the institutions to enjoy the sunlight, the open spaces and the caring nurturing environment that was now provided in the various centres. Sheltered workshops grew out of this period as the first shift/transition from institution to community.

In the mid 1970s through the 1980s and on, we find the 'open house' period. Largely influenced by the independent living movement, this is the time that we see the shift from classification systems and labeling to the enabling and empowerment of individuals. People with disabilities start to take charge of their own destiny and demand to be recognized as citizens with the same rights and privileges as everyone else. Of course, today we find the warehouse, greenhouse and open-house approaches are all alive and well, although the movement toward the open house continues!"

Recession creates a new breed:
the outplacement specialist

The deep recession of the early 1980s created a new category of career counsellors focusing on outplacement. The first Canadian employer to provide departing employees with outplacement services was the International Nickel Company (Inco). In the United States, services of this kind had been available to corporations since the early 1960s, ever since Humble Oil had asked New York retail career practitioner Saul Gruner to work with some employees who had become "redundant" and help them find other work. Several years later, Gruner partnered with Tom Hubbard to create a firm called Thinc, which became the first consulting firm devoted exclusively to a new human resources specialty that became known as outplacement consulting.

In the early 1970s, Inco had contacted Woods Gordon, a Toronto-based management consulting firm, and asked it to bring a service of this kind to Canada. Outplacement materials and programs were virtually non-existent but David Saunders and Robert Evans, the two consultants at Woods Gordon charged with the task, called Tom Hubbard for advice, which Tom readily gave, Evans recalls. They hammered together a program, ultimately providing more than one hundred Inco managers and professionals across the country with outplacement consulting, the first contract of its kind in Canada.

By June of 1975, Murray Axmith, a Toronto social worker turned management consultant, had changed his career path again and established Murray Axmith & Associates, the first Canadian company devoted exclusively to outplacement consulting. The following spring, the management consulting firm of Stevenson Kellogg, under the leadership of Eric Barton, established a specialized unit within its general consulting practice to focus on outplacement services.

In its early days in Canada, outplacement consulting services were provided only to senior executives and included the provision of office space and secretarial support. Outplacement consultants advised management on how to prepare for and handle termination meetings. They were on site to meet with employees after they had been fired to arrange for the career counselling services to begin. Conducted in one-on-one sessions, the counselling process was intensely personal and the service continued until the individual had found another position.

This rather exclusive service limited to senior executives began to change as the recession of the early 1980s deepened. Front line managers began firing staff. Few were familiar with the nuances of current legislation and they often handled these terminations poorly. Messy lawsuits for wrongful dismissal soon followed.

Stinging from bad press and expensive settlements, and driven by an overriding desire to stay out of court, corporations began to centralize human resources functions such as terminations, screening, recruitment, manpower planning and training. They also began looking for outside help before firing anyone.

"Corporations would come to us and say that they were going to have to release a lot of people, fifty people, one hundred people, in some cases, one thousand or more people," recalls Murray Axmith. "And they were very, very concerned about the impact of a large-scale termination and the news associated with that on the public perception of the company, and also on the people who remained in the company.

"They started to offer the service at levels beyond the executive level right down to the blue collar level. And we had to quickly revamp our programs so that we could accommodate that."

Revamping programs meant condensing the counselling process, no longer leaving it open-ended, until the individual found work. It also meant greater use of group counselling. "It was the only way of responding to the needs of a lot of people at the same time," Axmith says.

As well, it meant hiring and training outplacement consultants. Many of the people attracted to this new human resources specialty were not educated as counselling professionals but instead had backgrounds in diverse fields such as adult education, social work or sociology. Some had been members of the clergy. Others had backgrounds in recruitment, placement or training.

"At first we looked for people with applied behavioural science experience who also had business experience, which was an unusual animal to find," Axmith says. "After a time, we expanded our criteria and began to hire people who had a lot of empathy and sensitivity and who had superior interpersonal skills and business experience. Business experience was very, very important. If people didn't have it, they didn't understand the roles that people had in business."

The career and employment counselling services provided by the outplacement industry were similar in content to services being offered in the public domain, although they were made more challenging by the presence of two clients: the job seeker and their former employer.

"Strong ethics and standards for professional delivery were key to the success of the outplacement counselling process," said Axmith.

Labour responds to the post-industrial workplace

During the 1980s, many thousands of union members across the country lost well-paying jobs. Many did not possess the skills needed to take on the work being created in the industrial sector and had little hope of finding another job like the one they had lost.

With government programs strained to capacity and workforce development strategies still in gestation, the permanent displacement of so many union members and the impact on their families compelled the Canadian Labour Congress and its affiliated unions into action. Lobby efforts were mounted and unemployment committees began to look into the needs of unemployed members—in particular those considered redundant because of low skill levels.

Industrial labour adjustment programs were set up to provide information and guidance. Early access to such programs generally meant that individuals had greater confidence and made better choices. Displaced workers who took advantage of labour adjustment services also tended to find their way back into the workplace sooner.

New skills were often what reopened the door. Skills were the power of the craft unions early in the century, says labour educator D'Arcy Martin. "Skilled workers banded together and negotiated with skills as their main lever." With the advent of industrial unionism and its growth among unskilled workers, skills became "a management right, under a 'Taylorist' kind of production, under a system whereby you would check your brain at the door and implement instructions."

The pendulum had swung back, Martin observes. "If you're going to have anything that is responsive, that is fluid, that is knowledge-intensive, you're going to have to have workers who are capable of making decisions."

This meant training.

"You can't expect a worker, suddenly out of nowhere, to develop a self-concept and an autonomy and a capacity to judge. That has to be part of their lived work experience."

Pushed by new realities such as these, from some corners of Canada's labour movement, a training policy emerged. BEST (Basic Education and Skills Training) was designed to help union members deal with change and prepare for a more complex workplace.

Basic skills were defined as the "foundation skills" one needed to pursue further education and training. In labour's view, at least, reading, writing, numeracy and critical thinking were the skills people needed if they hoped to function successfully in their lives, communities and society at large.

Labour's approach was founded, in part, on the notion of "literacy for empowerment." By strengthening members' language skills, it was felt, unions would be responding to their real human needs. Such training was also seen as a way to make unions more relevant and to build their influence through the use of union instructors, materials and course content.

Oil rigs, outrage and "jobs, jobs, jobs"

Pierre Elliot Trudeau, as prime minister, was the kind of great and legendary figure people either loved or hated. By the time the signal year 1984 had made its debut, he had become the politician a majority of Canadians loved to hate, criticize and blame.

In the west they blamed him for the collapse of oil prices. Things had been going great in Alberta. Canada's Texas, sparse in population but gigantic in resources, had been growing like there was no tomorrow. The National Energy Program (NEP) placed restrictions on Canada's oil and gas industry. South of the border, the world's largest free market imposed no such restrictions and the oilrigs pulled up stakes and headed south.

After about a year of sparring, the Alberta and federal governments came to a compromise. By the close of 1981, multi-billion dollar mega-projects were promised for the Alberta tar sands. Petroleum prices were at record levels and were projected to rise continuously and indefinitely. As the recession took hold in early 1982 however, oil prices began to plummet and, by the spring of 1982, the mega-projects collapsed as markets disappeared for the province's heavy oil, which was expensive to extract from the tar sands.

The oil boom was bust. Western alienation was such that the cancellations of the mega-projects, which had reverberations throughout the economy, were blamed on the NEP rather than on international market forces.

Canadian oil companies, supposedly the prime beneficiaries of the ill-timed and luckless Liberal policy, "sank in the undertow of a collapsing Canadian oil industry. Floods of workers, drawn from the east by reports of Alberta riches," recalls historian Desmond Morton, "turned around and went home. Others stayed to join local hordes of unemployed."

In almost every part of the country, Pierre Trudeau was blamed for the numbers of unemployed, the shrinking dollar and a government that continued to spend while household incomes dwindled. Whatever the merits of the complaints, Trudeau's actions were restrained by the international recession of 1982 to 1984. It was February 29, 1984, Leap Year Day, when the beleaguered Trudeau took his famous walk in the snow and returned with a decision to retire, this time for good.

He left a vacuum.

Bay Street darling John Turner, who had been waiting in the wings, was anointed Liberal leader and then prime minister, only to become, within less than six months' time, a historical footnote.

Defining roles, providing options, and improving competency

While the demand for outplacement counselling grew, not-for-profit agencies and organizations rallied resources to battle unprecedented youth unemployment and colleges in eastern and western Canada introduced diploma programs for career counsellors and career practitioners.

CHOICES

Best known among Canadian career products is CHOICES, the first career information tool in the country to blend occupational information with personal data in an interactive computer program.

Information technology was still in its infancy when Phillip Jarvis, an ex-military personnel officer, began working as a researcher/writer in Ottawa's Occupational and Analysis branch. Stuart Conger was his boss.

"Early on in the game, I suggested to Stu that we put everything into a computer in a standardized format," Jarvis remembers. "We were targeting nearly seven hundred monographs of four pages each. And that was times ten provinces or territories, times two languages. It was boxcar loads worth of publications." Once the data was in the computer the magic of the combined power became obvious. "We managed to complete in three years what we had projected would take twelve years to do across the country," Jarvis says.

A tantalizing by-product of the Careers Canada and Careers Provinces series was an extensive database of Canadian occupational information, in both French and English. Jarvis and Conger began to look for ways to use it.

While their political masters endured the woes of power, government staff responsible for carrying out government policy in the workplace continued their attempts to make sense of a complex work world.

The national placement service envisaged by people like Etta St. John Wileman and Bryce Stewart, with its published information about employment opportunities and vocational counselling for young people, had long since become a reality. Stewart's yearned-for unemployment insurance had been around for over forty years.

The precise thrust and intent of Ottawa's role in the Canadian labour force continued to puzzle and confound. Some in the federal employment service still viewed it primarily as a placement operation, while others saw it as responsible for the labour market as a whole, with placement merely one of many interrelated functions.

Among these latter, the definition of the service's role in providing vocational guidance and career assistance was often as confused. Was its function to disseminate information about the labour market to help people make intelligent decisions? Or was it intended to assist individuals directly, by providing counselling and guidance?

In 1983, a series of internal studies, meetings and experimental "user trials" coalesced into a program that became known as the "revitalization" of the Employment Service. Increasingly, it was being recognized that there would never be enough resources to offer one-on-one services to all the unemployed. Interactive technology, it was felt, could facilitate a greater degree of self-service by allowing clients to find answers to questions without involving CEIC staff. Further, services would not be provided "that were already provided, or could be provided, in a competent way by private employment agencies, the personnel services of businesses or by other organizations." Counselling, for example, could only be offered where it "would not occur" in the absence of the employment service.

Elsewhere in Canada and the United States, computer-based information systems were in various stages of development. Jarvis visited some of them, hoping to find a system that would meet the government's needs. Instead, he discovered the computer information systems currently in use or in development were not at all interactive. "I knew we could go farther in interactivity," he says. "That we could have people talking directly on-line with computer systems, putting in their own information about their interests, temperaments and educational attainment."

Charged with the project of developing a system of this kind, Jarvis created CHOICES. "It is an information tool," he says, "designed to help counsellors do their jobs better." And interactive it is. CHOICES users sit at a terminal, put their own personal information into the system and explore and examine hundreds of occupations in search of those to which they are suited.

Early in the 1980s, the program added an educational and training file to allow users find training and educational information relevant to their occupational choices. A few years later, the government licensed CHOICES to a private concern. Within a month or so, Jarvis recalls, that same private concern came knocking on his door and he had to make his own career choice. He decided to move into the private sector to further develop the CHOICES program.

Instead of trying to be all things to all people, the EIC would "seek out niches in the labour market where it could make a difference."[4] Within this rather broad blueprint, it was decreed that federal government employment services would be divided into three categories. First, the government would continue to produce and distribute labour market information, improving the relevance and quality of the data offered and increasing the capacity of local offices to deliver it "to workers, employers, students, teachers and other groups."[5] Second, it would continue to operate and attempt to "streamline" the national Labour Exchange, which matched workers and jobs, using automation and a variety of self-service techniques. Third, and finally, it would provide "adjustment services," including counselling and training, to those Canadians most in need of them.

Increasingly, the services provided to individual clients coming through the doors of Canada Employment Centres were based on the needs of the individual. Under the broad rubric of "adjustment services," extensive funds were devoted to the development of new job search technologies, job creation programs, training initiatives and the provision of career counselling.

Interactive computer programs like CHOICES were valuable tools in an environment of widespread need and fiscal restraint. At the same time, one-on-one counselling sessions were increasingly replaced by group work.

Clients considered "job ready" were not even formally registered, but directed instead to take advantage of some of the government's new self-service features such as Job Boards and the National Job Bank. Individuals deemed not ready to look for work for one reason or another were passed along to a government employment counsellor. And anyone who was seen to need in-depth counselling was referred to appropriate community agencies and services.

Job-finding clubs had been introduced for Canadians receiving unemployment insurance benefits. Originally an American employment services project that had been developed to help ex-psychiatric patients find their way into the workplace, the idea had been adapted by CEIC and incorporated into a three-week training course in job search techniques.

Counselling from competent counsellors

In-house training had not always been available to government employees who provided counselling to the unemployed. Indeed, specific training in counselling techniques had not even been required until an internal directive issued in the mid-1970s reversed that.

The increasingly complex demands of the workplace, "and the effects of these demands on clients to adjust and adapt to issues such as changing expectations, redundant skills and sudden job loss have presented counsellors with constant and novel challenges," according to a government information paper published at the time.[6] In such an environment, there were concerns regarding the competency of counsellors.

There was a growing recognition that the people showing up in Canada Employment Centres were no longer just the hard-core unemployed. Firms began to flatten and fire swaths of middle managers; farms, fisheries and primary industries cut back operations or shut down; and long-term employees, industry specialists and professionals were also unemployed. Expertise to deal with clients as diverse as these was simply not readily available. It had to be developed. In spite of all the attention being given to labour market information, there was relatively little emphasis on the skills of the people providing that information on the front lines.

"What about counselling skills and counsellors?" asked Conger. "We had a policy that said that every unemployed worker who wants counselling and needs it will get it from a competent counsellor. So we instituted a staff training program, a competency-based staff training program. Counsellors had to take these courses, write exams and pass them."

Lyn Bezanson, a teacher and guidance counsellor who had found her way into the federal government, was one of the people responsible for developing the various modules that made up the training program. "We were extremely fortunate to be able to bring together some of the country's best theorists," says Bezanson, now Executive Director of the Canadian Career Development Foundation. "We worked with Phil Patsula from the University of Ottawa, Norm Amundson and Bill Borgen from the University of British Columbia and Vance Peavy, from the University of Victoria." Ultimately, hundreds of government employees took part in competency-based training programs throughout the 1980s.

By late in the decade, training of government employment counsellors slowed considerably. "We had trained almost everybody and we weren't getting in any new counsellors," explains Gayle Takahasi, a Toronto region employment counsellor and trainer with the CEIC, which was eventually to be renamed Human Resources Development Canada (HRDC).

In the shifts and changes that characterized government employment services in the 1990s, there would be even less demand for counsellor training amongst federal employees as the responsibility for counselling clients was passed to the provinces or contracted out to community-based agencies.

Nonetheless, the government's Competency-Based Training program developed a life of its own. Some of the training modules would eventually be incorporated into counsellor training programs at community colleges. The program would ultimately be translated into several languages and become one of the training programs that Canadian government officials marketed to other governments around the world.

Career education — an emerging specialty

In the volatile economic climate of the 1980s, as youth unemployment soared and the school-to-work transition became a hot political potato, the process of counselling young people about their potential working lives began to command greater attention from both federal and provincial governments.

Ever so slowly in Canada's educational system, career education had begun to move beyond its roots in vocational and technical education. Responding to growing needs by working to build the acceptance of career education, was a small group of dedicated career educators who began to make their presence felt in the country's high-school guidance community.

Some guidance teachers found their way into government and began to influence the growth of career education from behind the scenes. Others moved out of education into the business community. Still others stayed within the educational system and began to develop career guidance programs.

Canada's educational policies differed from province to province, reflecting the unique economies and labour markets overseen by provincial governments. The country's more than sixteen thousand elementary and secondary schools were governed by elected school boards, largely independent agencies within each province and territory. Although directives came from provincial ministries of education, only a few school boards had mandatory career guidance courses and the vast majority viewed guidance services as optional. Only a few provincial educational ministries provided funds for guidance services, virtually all of it for teachers' salaries.

Quebec was the only province in Canada with a specific, clearly defined career guidance program, articulated during the Quiet Revolution of the early 1960s. In every school in Quebec, there was a licensed vocational guidance counsellor, often supported by other staff.

In other provinces, even though there were guidance counsellors in most schools, all of whom were licensed teachers, only a few had a special interest in career education. Guidance came into schools in English Canada as a staff position, but without an organizational structure to support it. As a result, the services provided students tended to vary from location to location; for the most part they focused on personal guidance rather than career guidance and often were based on the interests and proclivities of the teachers assigned guidance duties.

In certain pockets of the Canadian educational system, however, the influence of a few teachers and guidance counsellors with a strong interest in career education was felt. At times, the innovation originated with the provincial government, as it had in Alberta, which had created a specific government department charged with preparing the province's labour force for the world of work. As part of its mandate, this department published career and employment information and developed programs and courses that were made available to the province's educators.

Nova Scotia's government took an early and keen interest in career guidance according to ex-guidance teacher turned provincial employee Kathie Swenson, who worked for Nova Scotia's ministry of education. "The Minister of Education didn't believe in school counsellors," she recalls. "[The Minister] thought they were masquerading as shrinks and

> **Innovations in career development in a university-based setting**
> Career counselling and placement services were established at Memorial University in St. John's Newfoundland in the 1960s, made possible by early funding from the Counselling Foundation of Canada. In the 1990s, the university entered into a partnership with the federal government to assist the centre in broadening its focus from primarily placement to offering a wider rage of employment services. Building upon its original concept of a student-based model of service provision, and having merged with the Cooperative Education Services Centre, the centre has evolved to become the Department of Career Development and Experiential Learning. The department both delivers services and undertakes research and is strengthened by partnerships with the community and industry.

was prepared to strike them off with the stroke of a pen. The only way we were able to maintain any status for counsellors in the schools was to say they were career counsellors and that meant a tremendous change in direction. It was a hard sell, not only to the minister but we then had to go out and convince guidance counsellors who very much enjoyed the personal counselling and who now were going to have to put a different slant on things. We also had to provide training programs and professional development and develop new curriculum guidelines on career counselling."

In Ontario, innovation and program development often happened through the efforts of individual teachers with a strong interest in the field. Career education, as defined in the 1980s by Ontario's Ministry of Education, was a regional cross-curriculum approach, which encouraged links with the community. This was significantly impeded by the insistence of the teachers' union that career counselling could only be conducted by certified teachers (without any particular knowledge of the career development field).

The Toronto Board of Education approached Toronto's Youth Employment Services (YES) and asked to share its expertise in working with young people. A Pre-Employment Training Program with manuals and teachers' training guide was produced and made available to some of the teachers in the Toronto area.

By the middle of the 1980s, the number of Canadians with university degrees had multiplied by ten since 1951. And most universities had diversified their curricula to meet the diversity of demand.

Quebec offered specific graduate studies in career guidance in a couple of its universities. In the rest of the country, the faculties of education were the primary source of training for counselling professionals. Most of the programs were designed for guidance counsellors within the school system, and personal and social counselling was the main focus. Only a course or two in career or vocational counselling was available, as a rule.

Academic research in the career counselling field in English Canada was almost unheard of. The Canada NewStart program had generated research activity in the 1960s and '70s, but little of consequence had been undertaken since.

Professor Norm Amundson from the University of British Columbia (UBC) recalls that he approached the field of career counselling somewhat reluctantly. "I ran the other way," he says, with a chuckle. "In the field of psychology, there's a hierarchy and career and vocational psy-

Canadian Association of Career Educators and Employers (CACEE)
The first professional association dedicated to the career planning needs of post-secondary students in Canada was established in 1945 as the University Advisory Services. Today known as the Canadian Association of Career Educators and Employers (CACEE), it was founded through the initiative and support of representatives from the Universities of British Columbia, Toronto, Western Ontario, and Sir George Williams (now Concordia), and the Department of Veterans Affairs. Initially an effort to re-integrate veterans onto Canadian university campuses and subsequently into the world of work, CACEE's strength over the years has resulted from the breadth of its membership base. CACEE includes both career educators who work in colleges and universities across the country and employers who recruit students and graduates from campuses across Canada. It has been instrumental in the enhancement of the profession, by providing professional development opportunities in the field, developing career planning and job search publications and services to meet the needs of students, providing resources to its membership to help facilitate the link between employers and students and in contributing to the establishment of standards for the profession.

chology was the lowest form. So at first I wouldn't touch it with a ten-foot pole. There was very little creativity attached to the field in the 1970s," he explains. "It had this bureaucratic image, of people in brown suits and worn-out shoes, with ties askew, sitting in an office all day, giving people reams of tests and making pronouncements. There wasn't much energy, creativity or imagination. And for most people who were in psychology, it didn't have much appeal."

Amundson's interest was piqued by Jean Claude Coté, who worked in Ottawa at the federal employment service. He asked Amundson and Bill Borgen, both of UBC, to turn their academic gaze on the ways and means of working with groups of unemployed people. Their report, "The Dynamics of Unemployment," funded by the Social Science Research Council and published in 1984, had an impact on the field as well as establishing Amundson and Borgen as leading thinkers in it. It was the first documentation in Canada of the emotional roller coaster that people ride after losing their jobs and the grieving that often accompanies such a loss.

The pragmatic, rational approach taken in job finding clubs prior to Amundson and Borgen's work was relevant in many instances, Amundson says. "A lot of people need information and some practical assistance to learn how to look for work. But for others there's more to it than that, there's a lot of emotion. And the practical, rational models that existed couldn't handle it."[7]

> The Canadian Career Development Foundation (CCDF) was established in 1979 as a charitable Foundation to advance the understanding and practice of career development. Each year, CCDF awards up to $7,500 to a project/projects which demonstrate potential advancement of career development.

By the end of the 1980s, across the country, a growing number of academic researchers had begun to turn their attention to the field. Amundsen and Borgen would go on to research and write about the career field. In addition to the NATCON papers published each year after the National Conference, Canadian educators scholars who have added to the body of Canadian career literature includes Norm Atkinson, Lyn Bezanson, Bill Borgen, Colin Campbell, Gerald Cosgrave, Bryan Hiebert, Chris Magnussen, Bill O'Byrne, Phillip Patsula, Vance Peavy, Dave Redicopp, and Marilyn Van Norman.

Stuart Conger had retired from government life and was thinking about going back to university, he says, when Andre Pacquin, who had become the Director of the Employment Counselling Directorate in its Ottawa headquarters, approached him with a request. The department's Associate Deputy Minister wanted a proposal outlining ways in which the government's employment counselling training program could be extended nationwide for counsellors in other agencies. "It was Andre's idea that research and development be added."[8]

The idea of promoting career-focused research and development in the academic community held considerable appeal for Conger, who believed that with the right collaborative approach and enough money, Canada's university researchers could be galvanized to action. Once they had turned their fine minds to the task, new career programs, curricula and products would be created to address some of the complex issues that confronted Canadian workers at the end of the industrial era.

Conger brought together three academics from different parts of the country to work with him to develop a working paper: Vance Peavy, from the University of Victoria; Conrad LeCompte from the University of Montreal; and from the University of British Columbia, Bill Borgen. At a two-day think tank hosted by Employment and Immigration Canada and chaired by Peavy, the working paper was presented to scholars from both the anglophone and francophone communities, to practitioners in the field, government representatives and a range of people from different disciplines.

The resultant project—Creation and Mobilization of Career Resources for Youth (CAMCRY)—funneled $7.4 million from the federal coffers to the Canadian academic community, earmarked for research and development projects designed specifically to examine the needs of the country's youth for improved career counselling.

By the early 1990s, some forty-one projects were under development at fifteen Canadian colleges or universities. As with any major project with millions of federal dollars, from the beginning controversy swirled around CAMCRY. Nonetheless, says Vance Peavy, CAMCRY was a "valuable initiative. It provided funding to a large number of projects. Not all those projects turned out to be good or worthwhile, but many of them did. And it elevated the status of the field in Canada and gave career counselling and guidance a higher profile."

Community colleges begin to train career and employment counsellors

As the 1980s continued their turbulent course, more people began to move from one counselling-related sector to another and from one area of the country to another, cross-fertilizing the field as they did. Some found their way into career counselling through adult education or social work or workers' rehabilitation services. Others, like Bill O'Byrne, entered the field through community-based, not-for-profit agencies such as the YMCA, which offered employment and career services.

O'Byrne's career path took him out of community-based agencies into private practice and from there into the post-secondary education system as a community college professor. In 1986, the Ontario Ministry of Education and the Council of Regents approved that province's first diploma program for career and employment counselling practitioners at Sir Sanford Fleming College in Peterborough, Ontario. The curriculum was written by an advisory group brought together by O'Byrne and the first thirty students accepted into the program began their studies in September 1987.

About the same time, in Alberta, a similar program was put forward by Barry Day, who had become the Director of Training Services for Alberta Career Development and Employment. About five thousand people in the province had something to do with career development,

Interestingly it was often out of these community-based programs that resources would be developed to enhance the profession of career counsellors in Canada. For instance, in the mid-1990s, the Ontario Association of Youth Employment Counselling Centres published a handbook entitled Community Career and Employment Counselling for Youth: Principles and Practice. Grounded in a community-based model, the OAYECC document provided a standardized approach to service delivery, plus all sorts of strategies and ideas that counsellors serving other parts of Canada or other communities could adapt.

Day recalls, and outside of a course or two in the graduate programs in the educational psychology departments of Alberta's universities, there was little training available to them.[9]

At his boss' suggestion, Day decided to take a leave of absence. He brought together a team of keen young psychologists to consider the situation. Within a year, a curriculum had been developed and the Centre for Career Development was established at Edmonton's Concordia University College.

In the years since, community colleges in various parts of the country have added career development and counselling diplomas and certificate programs to their academic offerings through part-time, full-time and, in some instances, distance education. In Regina, the Federated Indian College offers a certificate program for native and community counselling. Today in 2002, career practitioners are choosing from over seventeen college certificate/diploma programs and over thirty-one courses/programs of study at Canadian Universities.

Through the efforts of people like Frank Lawson, Gerald Cosgrave, Vance Peavy and Myrne Nevison, a new breed of career practitioners had emerged. Some had training in counselling and educational psychology and were beginning to find their way into the workplace, into community college and university counselling centres, into private training schools and not-for-profit agencies and even, in a few cases, into organized labour's "help centres."

[1] Desmond Morton, *A Short History of Canada* (Toronto: McClelland & Stewart, 1992).
[2] John Hunter, *The Employment Challenge* (Ottawa: Government of Canada).
[3] Ibid.
[4] Ibid.
[5] Ibid.
[6] "Information Paper on the Competency-Based Training Program in Employment Counselling for Employment Counsellors" cited in Canivet research paper, "History of Career Counselling.

CHAPTER 10

Recessionary
TIMES LEAVE A
Changed
Workplace
AND WORKER

B y the end of the 1980s, government budgets were seriously strained and "deficits compounded from year to year created large debt loads that had to be financed through loans from financiers." In the neo-conservative mood of the day, post-war goals of social security and full employment were replaced with "policies designed to increase global economic competitiveness through decreased government spending and reduced deficits," recalls historian Alvin Finkel.

So powerful had multinational corporations become that they were frequently able to "extract favourable conditions from governments of western nations eager to prevent jobs from being exported to other countries," Finkel notes. "Corporate taxes were cut" by such governments, "trade union protection reduced, environmental regulations relaxed and social programs cut"—all in order to secure corporate investment.

Like that of virtually every other country in the industrialized west, Canada's economic growth had shrunk to a fraction of the rates posted in the buoyant post-war era. Opportunities for work had been disappearing at an alarming rate and few were the families who had not had some experience of unemployment. By mid-decade, while the economy was on the mend in southern Ontario and Quebec, "the recession persisted grimly in much of Atlantic Canada and remained as a cruel affront in the recently buoyant west."

At the same time, overfishing was rapidly killing the Atlantic fisheries and a poor wheat crop in the prairies "was hardly worth marketing while the subsidised growers of Europe and the United States pursued their trade war." In his first post-election budget, Finance Minister Michael Wilson imposed drastic cuts on crown corporations, reduced pension benefits and imposed the much maligned Goods and Services Tax.

The end of "old certainties"

In just fifty years, from the dire days of the Great Depression to the employment upheaval of the 1980s, the workplace had gone through several complete transformations. At every stage, the increasing need for diverse and sophisticated guidance had spurred a process of inspiration and innovation by individuals within the institutions that were required or which saw it as their role to respond.

It was a radically changed workplace, as an increasingly anxious workforce was in the process of discovering. Workers might be better equipped and more highly educated than ever before, but in an age of economic uncertainty and ongoing workplace upheaval, the fact remained that people and technology frequently sparred for jobs.

Throughout the western world, many industrialized countries were facing similar situations. Old certainties were vanishing in an inundation of high tech newness and, with every wave of change, work and the way people did it changed as well. Career and labour market awareness were fast becoming a global necessity for institutions everywhere.

The federal government responded by creating the Canadian Labour Force Development Board (CLFDB) but eventually this was disbanded in favour of a further devolution to the provinces.

As the 1980s drew to a close, in the currents and crosscurrents of interactivity between the institutions of education, government, labour and not-for-profit agencies, the diverse and fascinating field of career counselling was gradually taking shape. Career education, career training and career counselling, all virtually unheard of half a century earlier, had evolved and developed into an identifiable form—a complex, interconnected, nationwide, career-related community of professionals with a growing commonality of purpose.

Skills and youth and the gap between two economies

By 1990, the Canadian economy was again in deep recession. Although the downturn was widespread throughout the western world, it was even more severe in Canada than in most other countries.

Many long-established companies simply collapsed, while among those that remained, mergers, acquisitions and large-scale restructuring were rampant, often including "drastic 'downsizing' that reached into the executive offices and emptied whole floors of the computer-literate information handlers who had held the future in their hands." In the short span of two to three years, literally hundreds of thousands of jobs were lost. "Experts blamed a lack of global competitiveness, an underperforming economy, even high taxes," writes Desmond Morton.

Whole corporate empires collapsed, and long-established retail chains dissolved into liquidation, as huge warehouse operations, often

U.S.-based, overturned the merchandising industry. To anyone opposed to the Canada-U.S. pact, however, the culprit was clearly Free Trade. Supporters of the deal argued that the recession was to blame for the disappearing jobs. With or without Free Trade, they said, the economy "was merely making the necessary adjustments to survive in an increasingly competitive environment."

It was the type of work one did, according to Toronto economist, Nuala Beck, which determined how vulnerable one was in the workplace. In Beck's view, the North American economy had been forced to restructure as a result of an inevitable economic shift that had occurred in the early 1980s. While economic growth since the First World War had been fueled by mass manufacturing, she said, a great deal had changed when, beginning in 1981, technology became the primary engine of economic growth.

STAY IN SCHOOL

Running at roughly 30 percent in these years, the unemployment rate among high school dropouts was more than double the percentage of youth unemployment as a whole. Nonetheless, as countless others had before them, young people continued to drop out of school for all sorts of reasons. Canada's high school dropout rate, having declined earlier in the decade, was again on the rise. Youth unemployment remained high. Young people who stayed in school and then carried on to post-secondary education had significantly lower rates of unemployment than those who dropped out before finishing high school.

Quebec had the highest rate of "school leavers," as they were called, just over 37 percent. Alberta, Ontario, British Columbia and Nova Scotia were not far behind.

As often as not, whatever the province, young people dropped out because they had not done particularly well as students and, at sixteen or seventeen, "finally" felt they could take their lives into their own hands. Many believed that nobody cared whether or not they finished their education.

Convincing young people like these that parents, teachers, employers—society itself—actually cared about the educational level they attained was a primary objective of the federal government's Stay in School initiative. It was "aimed at informing young people about the importance of education and training and the direct relationship between education and training and labour market prospects," said Paul Boisvenue, a senior official in the federal employment service.

A special department for youth concerns was established within the federal employment bureaucracy and a five-year national strategy was implemented with major initiatives centred on youth and their career and employment needs. High school mentoring and tutoring programs were set up. Young people were asked to become peer counsellors and participate in support groups for other students. Parents were encouraged to become more involved in school life.

To support the program, career awareness and career choice materials were developed and distributed each year during Canada Career Week, which was given a higher profile to encourage communities to organize career fairs and special career and employment events each fall.

Federal and provincial partnership arrangements were encouraged and a Canadian Career Information Partnership was established to bring together representatives from the various provinces to share ideas and materials related to youth and labour market issues.

In mass manufacturing or resource extraction, which Beck defined as the "old economy," people were seen to be at far greater risk of finding themselves on the chopping block. "My research shows that if you're employed in the old economy," Beck wrote in her book *Shifting Gears*, "the odds are better than 50 percent that your job will disappear."

New work was available during these years of restructuring and re-engineering, Beck pointed out, despite the dreary unemployment statistics. Where it was to be found, however, was in the "new economy," fueled by technology and centred in industries like computers, semiconductors, telecommunications, instrumentation, and health and medicine. People working in and looking for work in industries such as these would have a far easier time building successful careers and working lives.

According to Beck, the western world had experienced several different economic cycles since the middle of the 19th century. Every time an economic cycle shifted, there were new demands for higher level skills.

"Back in the Industrial Revolution," Beck observed, "the vast majority of workers had just a few years of elementary school; they could write their name, read simple sentences and add simple numbers. With skills like these, they had a leg up on everybody else.

"In the mass manufacturing era, we upped the ante. It wasn't enough to have a grade school education. The message was loud and clear. Get a high school diploma and you'll have a job with a future, you'll have a leg up. And once again, we've upped the educational ante. Industries with a future are knowledge-based industries, industries in which you're paid to think, not just to do. Industries now have a strong demand for high level skills and education."

As it had at the turn of the century, the workplace was splitting itself. Ninety years earlier, society was divided among agriculture, skilled crafts and upstart industry. Now, in the post-industrial '90s, the split was between manufacturing and the exploding field of technology.

On the one side, there was a rapid disappearance of jobs, as technology took on more work. On the other, jobs were being created, although not in equal numbers, in a burgeoning market demanding ever-higher level skills. From the broad-backed labourers of the early 1900s to the technologists, systems analysts and software specialists of the information era, the job descriptions had changed and changed again. And so had the requisite skills.

Community agencies and organizations, often the service delivery network closest to those most economically marginalized including youth and newcomers, developed new resources and techniques to respond. Youth organizations developed models of service delivery to accommodate an insatiable demand. Immigrant serving agencies developed Mentoring Programs linked to career coaches for foreign trained professionals (Skills for Change, Toronto). Junior Achievement of Canada developed a new board game "The Economics of Staying in School" which was introduced in classrooms in British Columbia, Alberta, Saskactewan, Manitoba and Ontario.

In circumstances such as these, workers of every age and level of the workplace were vulnerable, but none more so than the young. With fewer manufacturing jobs available, and more positions requiring higher skills, it was difficult for newcomers to get a start. Post-secondary education made it somewhat easier, "but even this proved no guarantee," notes Alvin Finkel. "Lifelong employment with a single company became increasingly uncommon and young workers often had to be content with short-term contracts followed by a new intensive job search."

Although few articulated it at the time, Canadian youth had slowly become aware that the world of work was changing, that technology was, in part at least, the driving force behind that change and that traditional expectations of job security were breaking down.

A landmark poll of Canadian youth done in the '80s had surveyed the values, beliefs, personal concerns and relationships of young people between fifteen and nineteen years of age. Some 3,600 Canadian youths responded to the questions of researchers Reginald Bibby and Donald Posterski. In their book, *The Emerging Generations, An Inside Look at Canada's Teenagers*, they write: "Teenagers go to movies and watch robots like R2D2 perform impressive feats and quickly compute that robots are more efficient than people for many of the jobs now and in the future.

"Listening to the news before supper, they hear that three hundred graduating lawyers and 1,350 new engineers face 'no vacancy' signs in their respective professions. Mentally they cross two further vocational options off their lists. They remember well how they wanted to work last summer but only found a job that paid the minimum wage and lasted for just two weeks."

Without a sense of the future, the report's authors wrote, discouragement settled on many of Canada's young people. As one sixteen-year-old told them: "Teenagers go to school for twelve years and when they get out of school they have to fight for work. And if they don't work they get labeled as young punks or lazy bums. It isn't their fault they can't find work. The government isn't helping them any."

Comments such as these no doubt frustrated government officials who had been attempting for years to find ways of meeting the needs of Canadian young people in the course of their transition from school to work. With demographics indicating unprecedented growth in Canada's Native youth population, attention began to once again focus on the development of programs specific to Canada's Native community.

Mahjetahwin Meekunaung Walk the Path - a Multi-media Career Learning Program

Serving the Anishinabek territory, the Anishinabek Career Centre offers career counselling and resources to First Nations peoples at all stages: children, youth, adults and elders. The Mahjetahwin Meekunaung program includes hosting a career fair, producing an educational video, providing an interactive website, developing a poster series that promotes career planning as part of an ancient process, in addition to providing opportunities for face to face career counselling. The Centre provides information on scholarships, training opportunities, role models (success stories) and how to start your own business (either on or off the reserve). It has also created a Circle of First Nations Career and Employment Practitioners, a network of resource people in the field who can share best practices and proven approaches.

Hurtin' for this job

By the mid-1990s, in anxious households throughout the country, the daunting issue of work, skills and unemployment had become an aching concern for many, frequently aggravated by immediate, close-to-home wounds. Throughout the Canadian workforce, regardless of age, gender or previous experience, the complex demands of the quick-change workplace were growing steadily harder to fathom.

In the office blocks and shopping malls of the industrial core, Out of

Scenes like this, with hundreds of job seekers lining up for a few positions, were a reality in some parts of Canada in the 1990s, harkening back to labour markets of decades before.

Business signs were coming down as the first flushes of life returned to the economy. The profit curves on the graphs in corporate reports were on the rise again and, based on the wisdom of years gone by, the number of jobs in the want ads should have been as well.

Instead, as business resumed its pell-mell pace and productivity soared anew, a very different pattern had begun to emerge in the job market. The jobs that were coming back had different specifications, in slimmed-down factories with half their previous number of employees. In the secondary job market, moreover, home of the part-time temp and the "McJob," workers were actually in demand.

Profitable and less successful businesses alike continued to shrink staff, always in the name of improved competitiveness. "That meant mergers, factory shutdowns and the introduction of technology, particularly computerization, all of which reduced demand for labour," writes Alvin Finkel. "Robots often replaced assembly line workers, traditional 'women's jobs' vanished as voice mail and electronic mail replaced many secretaries and automated banking reduced the need for tellers."

What this all turned out to mean was that although the leading economic indicators settled back into the positive percentiles, higher ongoing levels of unemployment began to be thought of as normal, as did longer periods out of work for those unfortunate enough to find themselves among the unemployed.

The "jobless recovery" was the name it was given by the media. Increasingly, the unemployed included displaced workers at all skill levels throughout the ranks of industry as well as the gigantic service sector. There were jobs, to be sure, there were even "good" jobs for those who had the skills but, for a significant part of the workforce, there were few opportunities.

The dilemma was crystallized one sub-zero day in early 1995, in a scene truly reminiscent of the Great Depression. The General Motors plant in Oshawa, Ontario was said to be considering adding a third shift, a move that would create as many as one thousand new jobs if the company followed through. On the strength of this rumour and nothing more, fifteen thousand people stood outside in the depths of winter just to put their names on a list.

There was no promise of interviews. The company was simply compiling names of people who might be interviewed if the jobs were created. "I haven't worked for almost three years, except for odd jobs through Manpower," said unemployed electrician Paul Little, age twenty-nine, in a *Toronto Star* article on January 25, 1995. "I've got four children. I'd do anything for a job at GM."

"Hopefully this line leads to employment," was the way twenty-seven-year-old Brian Scarlett put it. "I'm unemployed, I'm on welfare, I'm hurtin' for this job." Scarlett and the thousands of others who stood in line in Oshawa were the literal embodiment of a state of

Whether it was fifteen thousand shivering outside GM, four thousand in an Air Canada office, or three thousand people at a food store opening in Windsor, Ontario, in pursuit of one hundred and twenty jobs, Canadians were waiting in line, physically and mentally, in the vain belief that the "good jobs" of days gone by were coming back.

mind that had become prevalent among workers across the country. Whether it was fifteen thousand shivering outside GM, four thousand in an Air Canada office, or three thousand people at a food store opening in Windsor, Ontario, in pursuit of one hundred and twenty jobs, Canadians were waiting in line, physically and mentally, in the vain belief that the "good jobs" of days gone by were coming back.

And for many who were hurtin', it was not just a case of a "good job," but any job at all.

A U-turn in workplace policy

As Ottawa scaled back its presence in the Canadian economy to 1950 levels, everything, it seemed, was on the chopping block—from literacy training to environmental conservation efforts to industrial subsidies. As the government changed the ways in which it was involved in Canadian society, by reconfiguring programs or withdrawing services altogether, huge numbers of jobs disappeared. Among the ranks of those who remained, salaries had already been frozen and would remain so for years to come.

It was a carefully planned and executed strategy, designed to tackle the problem of government overspending head-on—and along the way to please the voters. And it worked. Through such procedures, in a matter of just three years, 45,000 public service jobs were eliminated; whole departments were wiped out.

Nowhere was the impact of the restructuring more pronounced than in the government's giant employment service. An extensive internal reorganization had been underway for years, under Minister of Employment Lloyd Axworthy, who had been named, following the 1993 election, to a portfolio he had held in the Trudeau years.

Human Resources Development Canada (HRDC) had been the government's way of concretizing a grand vision—a comprehensive labour force and labour market policy. The brutal reality, however, of a $1 billion cut that was announced early in the Liberal mandate had meant that, whatever the scope of the vision, the operational and management funds available to put it into practice had been sliced by more than a third.

Unemployment Insurance was reborn as Employment Insurance (EI) as benefits and entitlements were cut and qualifying criteria tightened. However necessary the change of direction, however long overdue the tightening of public purse strings, the cuts came at a time when individual needs for help and direction in the Canadian workplace were acute. After years of jobless recovery, high unemployment, restructuring, downsizing, mergers, acquisitions and shutdowns, the world of work had become a complex, volatile and threatening place.

Gaps within gaps

Within five years of the Chretien government's election, Ottawa's spending on social programs had decreased by more than $10 billion a year. In those same years, real income had declined in three out of five Canadian households.

THE NOC AND CAREER HANDBOOK

The National Occupational Classification (NOC) was developed by HRDC staff under the direction of JoAnn Sobkow, Margaret Roberts and the late Lionel Dixon. It was implemented in 1993 as a replacement for the Canadian Classification and Dictionary of Occupations (CCDO). An extensive program of research, analysis and consultation with employers, workers, educators and associations as well as providers and users of labour market data ensured strong links between the NOC and Statistics Canada's parallel Standard Occupational Classification.

The NOC represents a new approach to occupational classification.

The objective for the NOC was more ambitious. The NOC developers wanted the new

While a bare majority of people still enjoyed the relative security of full-time, permanent jobs, for a great many working people, economic uncertainty had become a fact of life. Savings accounts were depleted and, in record numbers, Canadian individuals and businesses were giving up and declaring bankruptcy.

Stagnating earnings, chronic unemployment, persistent under-employment, the computerization of work, and a workplace split between low-skilled service industry jobs and high-skilled "knowledge work" all tended to compound the problem. A flurry of reports by social commentators, religious organizations, policy-makers and think-tanks drew attention to a steadily widening gap, not only in levels of affluence, but also in opportunities, skills and even hours spent on the job.

Most in demand and best equipped to establish themselves successfully in the world of work, the reports revealed, were Canadians who were well-skilled, well-trained, astute and forward-thinking. Lagging far behind were those who had become overwhelmed by change, people who resisted training and re-training, and people who, in some cases, feared and resented the new technology and its demands in the workplace.

For many of those who had fallen behind, the only alternative to unemployment was temporary, part-time or short-term contract work, lumped by Statistics Canada under the catch-all label, "non-standard employment." Some people actually preferred work of this kind, of course—many of them women, especially working mothers. Since the 1970s, in fact, as women continued to move into the Canadian workforce in ever greater numbers, their needs for flexible working arrangements had become a major factor in the ongoing re-definition of work.

But by the mid-1990s, the widespread increase in non-standard work had less to do with women's needs than it did with those of employers intent upon cutting costs. "Generally-speaking," observed a 1997 study by the Canadian Policy Research Networks think-tank, "non-standard work falls into the 'bad jobs' category: low pay, few benefits, little or no job security and few intrinsic rewards." In the cost-conscious '90s, as full-time "good jobs" continued to disappear, such non-standard "bad jobs" were cropping up in droves.

For large numbers of young people "in an environment of great job insecurity," the Advisory Committee on the Changing Workplace

classification to provide a map of the world of work that would help labour market analysts, researchers, counsellors, students and educators understand not just the content of occupations, but also the relationships between occupations. These relationships were to be based upon empirical rather than theoretical observations. The NOC Matrix provides a framework for understanding the functioning of the world of work.

HRDC also developed the Career Handbook, which is organized according to the NOC structure and relates work to people by providing ratings and descriptions of a wide variety of worker traits such as aptitudes and interests. It was designed to facilitate career counselling and exploration.

concluded, "the stages of life their parents took for granted—buying a home, starting a family—loom as intimidating, risky, long-term decisions if not completely out of reach."

Again, reduced benefits were denounced as a primary cause of financial distress among young Canadians. The school-to-work transition had never been easy, particularly for those without skills or adequate education. EI reforms had dramatically increased the amount of time on the job required to qualify for coverage and many young people found they simply could not accumulate enough working hours between one short-term job and the next.

In this toxic mix of chronic unemployment, income stagnation, polarization, skills gaps and lean, mean management, the Canadian workplace was becoming a very unforgiving place. It was a rare household that did not have a least one person in some degree of career distress...be it a breadwinner who was rarely home in time to share the evening meal, a part-time worker struggling to make ends meet, a young person just starting out or a mature, experienced worker struggling to start over.

Shifting values and perceptions of work

Workplace specialists Gordon Betcherman and Graham Lowe observed in their 1997 essay, "The Future of Work in Canada," that "Transformations in the workplace are profoundly affecting individuals, families and communities. New technologies, economic globalization, high unemployment, declining job security, stagnant incomes, polarized working time, and work-and-family tension define the context of work for many Canadians...the changing world of work is often accompanied by a growing sense of anxiety."

Security in "a job well done" had been a fundamental of middleclass life for most of the past hundred years. Now, however, as the century drew to a close, such feelings grew ever more scarce. No longer tied to lifelong employment with a single firm, security had become largely a matter of self-sufficiency, based on an individual's ability to take full personal responsibility for success in the world of work.

"We are in a lurching kind of time," observed Carla Lipsig-Mummé, director of York University's Centre for Research on Work and Society, a time "when the things that we took for granted were related to each other—work and employment and national prosperity—are unhooked from each other."

© David Muir/Masterfile

The introduction and widespread adoption of computers – starting in the 1970s and continuing through to the turn of the new century – continues to have a tremendous impact on the everyday working lives of Canadians

Slowly, hesitantly, reluctantly, Canadians began to confront their preconceptions on the subject of employment. Old notions of work as a kind of entitlement, something created by someone else and made available to them, were breaking down and people were coming to accept the need to look at work in different ways. Even as the message sank in, however, most Canadians remained deeply concerned about the future of work, in particular the prospect of being without it.

What was underway was nothing less than a shift in the techno-economic paradigm: it was a time of rapid and profound technological and economic transition, when the turbulence of everyday life was actually a surface effect of disturbances underway at far deeper levels of society. New technology, global markets, new management practices and the computerization of work were all contributing to the uncertainty and angst, the increased polarization and even the growing distrust between employers and employees.

Not only were individual lives more turbulent in such a climate, the report said, "but the 'anchors' provided by existing social institutions become less and less effective in helping people adjust to changing times." New anchors needed to be put in place. To these ends, the Roundtable on the Future of Work called for "action on the part of all stakeholders in Canadian society," with government participation being central. "Leadership skills that fit with the culture of post-industrial society," were required and governments would "have to be brokers for the different interests in society, and catalysts for new partnerships and a revitalized social contract."

New forms of compensation and benefits, work sharing, limitations on overtime, even shortened workweeks could be investigated, as well as new forms of worker representation for those outside the scope of collective bargaining.

Education and training—no panaceas in themselves, given the number of Canadians who were underemployed or unable to find work "even though they have skills to offer in the marketplace"—were nonetheless essential. Labour market information was required "to inform people about what types of skills to invest in and where to acquire them." Improved funding mechanisms were needed, along with more effective use of information and communication technologies for delivery of education and training services. It was clear, wrote the authors, that "investment in human capital is increasingly the best personal strategy for individuals and the best collective strategy for nations." Ultimately, what was needed to overcome the country's various skills gaps was "explicit recognition that the development of the world's best education and training system is a national priority.

"We can never expect to immunize ourselves from change," said the report. But "the goal of fuller (let alone full) employment has simply not been a high priority in Canada over the past decade or so. Instead, the emphasis has been on inflation and, more recently, public debt." These policies, while successful in achieving their immediate objectives, had also contributed to higher unemployment rates.

The furor over work and the workforce was a sore point for the Liberal government. As far as the prime minister was concerned, much of the criticism was unfounded. Close to 700,000 jobs had been created since he took office and the national unemployment rate was 9.5 percent, down from 11.2 percent in 1993.

The workplace, with all its woes and controversial problems, was the arena in which Jean Chretien's government was most vulnerable. In the media, as in the daily question period and his increasingly frequent visits to various parts of the country, all the prime minister ever seemed to hear about was jobs. Jobs, jobs, jobs. But by April, the employment

© Larry Fisher/Masterfile

statistics had begun to improve. Over 60,000 jobs had come on the market in the previous month and unemployment had dropped almost two full percentage points since 1994. An improving job picture was exactly what the Liberals had been waiting for. According to the polls, their popularity in the country was high. The opposition was extremely fractured. They gambled on the early election and issued an election call for June 2. The Liberals were victorious once again, although the results

Increased mechanization and the introduction of robotics has displaced industrial workers in all parts of Canada, but also created new jobs inthe high-technology industry emphasized the regional fragmentation of political support.

The federal government was in conflict with itself, pointing the way to a knowledge society with one hand and struggling to clear up a crisis in its active intervention policy with the other. Yet on Parliament Hill the mood was upbeat, with the Liberals winning a historic third term with a very comfortable majority of 172 seats in the 301 member House of Commons.

At century's end, there was no shortage of conflicts, crises and failures to preoccupy professionals in the career counselling field. The billions of dollars poured into the field of workplace management had furthered many valuable initiatives but the same lethal brew of stubborn workplace trends persisted—the same worrisome gaps in income, skills, age and gender. Devolution continued to sow confusion.

The realization that career counselling is not only for new entrants to the labour market, but also a service working people may require throughout their working life, has given rise to a specialization within the field known as the career coach. Like the rise in popularity of the personal trainer to assist people in realizing their physical fitness goals, a career coach is both advisor and advocate for their clients, providing various types of assistance. Career coaches can be found within human resource departments of large organizations, not-for-profit agencies, in the private sector and on-line.

The complications of the workplace had grown enormously in the course of a hundred years, having a serious impact on the career counselling community. It may be argued this impact was positive as it propelled the growth of a broadly based group of career practitioners and encouraged niche specialties within the wider professional community.

THE VIEW AHEAD: THE
Profession
SPEAKS TO THE
Future

In observing the evolution of career counselling in Canada, one notices a convergence of four sectors of society: government, education, organized labour and the not-for-profit sector. Historically, government priorities have been to satisfy the economy's needs for skilled and productive workers. Educators, in turn have tried to provide opportunities for the acquisition of both knowledge and skills, to equip their students. The concern of organized labour was for workers' rights and protection from exploitation. And finally, the concerns of non-governmental organizations—or what has come to be known as the third sector, or civil society—involved the needs of individuals and their community.

In this case, "community" was defined in various ways. A geographical community, for instance a single industry town, could be grossly affected by an economic downturn, leaving those employed by primary industries, such as mining exploration or pulp and paper, bereft of income and social cohesion. At times like these, smaller centres became very reliant on the skills of its career counsellors to help displaced workers and their families adjust to being without work, to seek retraining or other options, and to deliver support programs to both workers and employers during the transition.

Community has also come to be defined by people who share a common characteristic. For instance, career counselling has become a significant part of the community of persons with disabilities. Employment programs of community organizations such as the Canadian Paraplegic Association, Canadian Hearing Society or Epilepsy Association, which assist those disadvantaged by a particular disability, or through post-war programs like the Workers' Compensation Boards, which facilitate the rehabilitation of people injured on the job, developed specialised approaches to career counselling that met the paticular needs of their client groups.

One of the most obvious "communities" in career counselling is those who serve newcomers to Canada. Originally part of the services offered by Settlement Houses which formed in the middle of the century, career counselling services to immigrants and refugees has become a specialized and sophisticated part of Canada's ability to replenish its workforce. Language testing and training, together with certification programs and other ways of validating the qualifications of newcomers, have again enriched the capacity of the profession to meet the needs of both the willing worker and the employer wishing to hire.

Employment equity legislation, developed in the 1980s and implemented widely within the public sector and to a lesser extent in the private sector, advanced employment programs and opportunities for those disadvantaged by market forces. Although controversial at the time of implementation, employment equity programs did spur on the development of refined counselling, assessment and placement tools that more accurately met the needs of those marginalized from gaining access to work.

Career counselling is a field that intersects almost every aspect of Canadian life. As you have read, again and again politicians have won—and lost—elections based on their capacity to satisfy the desires of Canadians for access to work. Jobs. Jobs. Jobs. It has been the career counselling community that has been able to bridge the gap: from school to training; training to work; employment to unemployment and back to employment again. Virtually every government department is concerned with some aspect of work: safety, excellence, health, education, competency and competitiveness. Similarly, within the private sector, the field of human resource development has become an increasingly sophisticated one. Job readiness and lifelong career planning continue to be the focus of community agencies and organizations which constitute the third sector across Canada. The tasks and skills of the career practitioner have had to keep pace with the ever-evolving demands of employers from every sector and job seekers from every community.

In contemporary life at the dawn of the 21st century, a phrase should be added to the old adage that there are two things in life a person cannot avoid: death and taxes…and a career transition…or two…or three.

Career as vocation

One of the benefits of affluence in Canada during the post-war period has been the shift from seeing work as simply a means of earning an income to understanding its potential role as a source of personal fulfillment and as a means of contributing to society. This shift in our understanding of the role of work in our lives mirrored the change we observed in the economy, where society no longer required every available worker to be engaged in meeting our most basic needs of food and shelter. But, in fact, as our economies grew and diversified, so did the work that went with them.

Although vocational counselling was an early part of the profession, initially it seems to have connoted a more limiting course of action leading to a job placement. In fact, at the close of the century the term "vocation" had come to carry a much more sonorous tone: suggesting one could be "called" to a unique, enriching work life through a vocation. Again, this may have only been the luxury of a certain segment of Canadian society, not an option for workers whose experience, skills and circumstances confined their work choices to a narrow set of options. But for others, particularly those able to afford post-secondary education in the latter third of the century, a vocation—or choosing work that some would say they loved—was a possibility, enhanced by the career counselling professionals' ability to assist in laying out the options.

In this sense, career counselling has itself become a vocation. Through the efforts of people like Cosgrave, Conger, Parmenter and Lawson, this critical societal function has become a coveted and hard won vocation of professionals operating in different settings and serving diverse communities across the country. Now understood as an essential part of a person's life—from their earliest school-aged years to beyond their retirement, where many Canadians continue to seek fulfillment through work even when their financial situation may not require it—career counselling goes part and parcel with our understanding of work in Canadian life. The career practitioner has a vital role in both the efficient functioning of the Canadian economy and in our societal life together, which affords people the opportunity to participate to the best of their abilities.

Cultivating a vision for the Canadian workplace had fallen initially to Etta St. John Wileman and then her successors throughout the century. The various stakeholders in the Canadian labour market, she had said, "must recognize their responsibility for unemployment and regard work as a social obligation, which has to be provided in order that both individual and the state may reap the benefit of constant regular productivity."

Today, after nearly one hundred years of development and growth, the venerable activist's vision still holds true.

This community comes of age

At the end of a century of momentous change, Canada's career counselling community has come of age. A national industry with roots throughout society, the field has acquired an identity. Scholars and educators now view it as a field of study and practice, one of direct relevance and value to the life of almost every Canadian worker.

The notion of a coming of age holds all sorts of important implications. It is a time of recognition, a time of opportunity and risk, a time of imminent change. For Canada's career practitioners, it is a time to examine the field as it has developed over the years and to work together to create a new vision of its potential in the years ahead.

In this new era, working Canadians will face significant challenges. In urban centres especially, the workplace is technical and highly specialized, the economy multi-layered and bewilderingly complex.

Abstract assets such as information and knowledge have become our nation's most valued commodities. Work life success demands a range of sophisticated skills: computer, math and literacy skills; and interpersonal and communication skills. In the smaller cities and rural centres, the availability of technology has made many traditional jobs obsolete, but at the same time has opened the door to innovation and excellence being produced in and exported from the most remote of communities.

For the most part, Canadians have risen to the challenge and today are as highly educated and skilled as workers anywhere in the western world. When they need help, these workers turn to professionals in the career counselling field—to career and employment counsellors, career information specialists and career practitioners.

Throughout the industrial era, work and life were largely considered as separate concerns. Work was the "job" to which one went for a specific time, then returned home, to take advantage of "leisure time." In the post-industrial society, although many people continue to work at jobs, the lines between work and life have become increasingly blurred. Work is brought into the home, into the car, often cutting into leisure time. As work has become a central aspect of Canadian life, people have begun to tread with care along the career path they chose to walk. Shifts have occurred in the demographic make up of the workforce, in occupational demands and in legislative mandates. The school-to-work transition has become much more difficult.

Theoretical perspectives have changed as well, shifting our basic understanding of how to help people know themselves and connect with their inner beings. In keeping with the tenor of the times, no longer is it a matter of "fitting the man to the job," but rather of fitting the "person" to the "work opportunity."

Career counselling at the start of the new millennium

A specific process to counsel others about their potential in the workplace first emerged in Canada in the 1940s. At the time, counselling was a one-time event, a battery of tests and assessments that were interpreted along psychological lines. These personal insights, it was hoped, would help people make appropriate work or educational choices.

Describing the career counselling process as "multi-faceted," Judy Hayashi of the Frank G. Lawson Career Centre at Dalhousie University in Halifax emphasizes the need to remain flexible in order to meet the different needs people have at different points in their lives. "At times," she says, "it is self-examination. At other times it is decision-making, information-gathering, and helping people understand and deal with change.

"There's another dimension," Hayashi adds. "Sometimes people get stuck, either because they have their own expectations and beliefs or they've picked them up. They feel pressured from family or culture or situations that are making them feel they can't decide or can't move in a certain direction. Then a lot of the focus needs to be on identifying difficulties and helping them to overcome those barriers."

Like most practitioners in the field today, Marilynn Burke, an educator and program developer with the Toronto District School Board, believes that career counselling is no longer "a point-in-time event. It is a process," she says, "an ongoing process, founded on self-examination, to help people build the knowledge and the skills they need to make good decisions and select appropriate, satisfying and meaningful roles throughout life."

"It facilitates individuals' understanding of all the dimensions of themselves," she believes. "Their interests, their skills, their personality and values, what motivates them, what's in their heart, what they feel passionate about and, of course, it includes knowledge of their opportunities."

A survey of practitioners and theorists in different sectors and different regions of the country reveals a wide range of views and perspectives on exactly what the process of career counselling is, what it should be and what it needs to offer to the people it serves. It is largely a "facilitation process," in the view of Gail Whitely, an employment counsellor with the Toronto District School Board. "Counselling is a journey from one point in time to another point in time which is in the future. It's something we create with our clients together. I'm not the expert on everything, but I do have some pieces that I can add to their process."

Counselling helps people "take a snapshot of where they are right now," says Whitely. "They look at their past and how that interacts. It helps them to take a step-by-step approach to get to wherever it is they want to get to, and hopefully to other resources. What we don't have, we find together."

At the end of the century that redefined work, some counsellors continue to rely on a battery of psychometric tests to "measure" an individual's abilities. In the complexity of the Canadian workplace, however, a high degree of self-knowledge, although important, is only part of the intricate puzzle of career decision-making and planning. Achieving work and life success has become far more demanding.

Attracted by growing needs such as these, enticed at times by research and development funds, new theorists and program developers have entered the field. New counselling methodologies and products have begun to appear. Many of the field's theorists and program developers are found in the world of academe, business and the not-for-profit sector.

Vance Peavy, professor emeritus at the University of Victoria and a self-described "independent scholar," views the counselling process as "a specialized situation where someone, the counsellor, attempts to help the person identify and understand and develop their capacities. Career counselling, all kinds of counselling," he says, "should be a capacity-developing process. If you don't know how to read, for example, then your options are definitely limited. If you learn to read, develop that capacity, then your options are expanded."

> Career counsellors must be "part analyst, part therapist, part teacher, part consultant, and hopefully, in the end, a friend."
>
> Elizabeth McTavish,
> former Counselling Director,
> The Counselling Foundation of Canada

Careers bring personal meaning

At the University of Lethbridge in southern Alberta, Kris Magnussen teaches counsellors in the Faculty of Education. Magnussen emphasizes the importance of personal meaning. In a masters program twenty years ago, he recalls, the primary career planning focus was, "in the test-them-and-tell-them category." This approach may have provided personal insight, Magnussen says, but testing alone was not always enough to motivate people to action. As he worked with clients, he says, he discovered "this big gap between what we could measure and the sense of connectedness that people had to what we were measuring."

Magnussen began to focus his attention on "the notion of meaning," developing a process of career counselling that concentrates on "helping individuals get meaningfully connected within their working life, in any one of the number of roles they play, from parent, to child to citizen." Meaningful engagement, is the key motivating factor, he believes. "If we cannot get people meaningfully engaged, we may as well forget the rest of it."

University of British Columbia's Norm Amundson, who also teaches career counselling, has a slightly different perspective. "A lot of people, when they have career issues, really have a problem in imagination," he says. "They can't imagine a new future for themselves." Career counsellors, Amundsen believes, must use their own imaginations to stimulate the imaginations of those who come to them for help. "Career counselling is problem-solving," he says, "but it's a whole lot more than that."

Bryan Hiebert from the University of Calgary feels strongly that career counselling should be seen as an educational and learning process more than a psychological one. There is "an emphasis in the career development field now," says Hiebert, "on client skills and generic skills and transferable skills. Clients come into counselling seeking to make some change in their life. It's the counsellor's job to help identify exactly how the client would like things to be different. And then to arrange with the clients the kinds of experiences that will actually help them learn the knowledge and skills that will help them make the changes that they want to make in their life. It ends up more of a teaching/learning enterprise."

Placing the emphasis on skills and learning gives people a sense of power and control over the process, Hiebert maintains. "As soon as you place it in a learning context, people realize that they're learning things all of the time and they realize that the reason they are having difficulty is that they haven't learned how to do it any better. That's quite an encouraging mes-

---

In Canada, the rate of unemployment for employable disabled people is extraordinarily high. According to the latest Statistics Canada figures, 48 percent of people with disabilities work. In contrast, 81 percent of non-disabled persons are employed.

A similar disparity exists with respect to post-secondary education. While only 6 percent of people with disabilities have university degrees, more than double this percentage of able-bodied people have a university degree.

DiscoverAbility was formed in 1991 as a partnership between The Hugh MacMillan Rehabilitation Centre and the North York Board of Education. These partners collaborated to establish a Career Assessment and Resource Centre for disabled students. DiscoverAbility provided programs and services ranging from career assessment to placement and in many cases, monitoring for post-secondary school registrants. Other partners included The Counselling Foundation of Canada, Canadian Banking Association, Wal-Mart and local colleges.

sage." Not only is it encouraging, he believes it can help reduce personal stress.

"When working with kids in schools, asking them what made them stressed, a recurring theme was, 'What do I do after high school?'" Hiebert says. "So the work I do in career development is a subset of the work I've been doing in stress. People are starting to understand the importance of having a plan for your life. They're starting to understand at an intuitive level that you're better off if you have an idea of what you want to do with your life rather than just playing it one day at a time."

"The word 'development' in The Concise Oxford Dictionary means a 'gradual unfolding,'" suggests Marilyn Van Norman, the Director of Student Services and the Career Centre at the University of Toronto, "and that is indeed what I believe career development has done over the years and will continue to do." The University of Toronto Career Centre has evolved into the world's largest university career service. Initiated in 1948 in response to the employment needs of veterans graduating from university, the centre now serves thousands of students each year.

"Those 1948 graduates probably went on to work for the same employer for thirty-five years," says Van Norman. "Today's centre, while still providing employment opportunities to students through a web-based on-line system, teaches students and recent graduates how to take responsibility for their own career." Called the Self-managed Career Development Model, this tool equips the graduate for their working future. "Graduates today will probably have four or five different careers and at least twice that number of employers," continues Van Norman.

> As the 1980s drew to a close, in the currents and crosscurrents of interactivity between the institutions of education, government, labour and not-for-profit agencies, the diverse and fascinating field of career counselling was gradually taking shape.

Career as part of the productivity equation

The perspective from those in the business community is somewhat more pragmatic. Edmonton psychologist, David Redekopp, puts his career counselling theories in business terms, looking at strategies and outcomes. "It's essentially the process of helping people think strategically about work and how that work interrelates with the rest of their life. You can't untie those two things, but it is a work focus. That's why it's called career counselling and not counselling. But the idea is to think strategically and to have some specific outcomes in place.

"You know, it is outcomes-based, it is not just process," says Redekopp, of the Alberta-based Life Role Development Group. "And if by the end of career counselling people have enough strategy by which to make their next moves and those moves are in a conscious direction, for the most part, career counselling has done its job."

Among the varied theories, philosophies and practices within the career counselling profession—strategic thinking, imagination, meaning, skill development, capacity building and good old fashioned "listening" —a healthy dialogue is underway. At the same time, a strong note of consensus often transcends the differences. Despite the seeming disparities in theoretical thought, a common thread runs through advanced career counselling theory at the beginning of a new era of work.

Content, programs and a shared vocabulary

Contact Point is an interactive Website (www.contactpoint.ca) committed to producing relevant and topical career information and to opening lines of communication throughout Canada's career counselling community. The website was created by a group of career practitioners – each practicing in a different setting – who came together to define their need for information and design how to access that information. In practice, and central to the Contact Point philosophy, the practitioner as user is both the provider and recipient of the information.

Launched into cyber space in January of 1998, Contact Point offers discussion groups, gateway listings, professional development listings, a searchable Resource Centre, job postings, bursary applications, a quarterly newsletter, monthly circulars and special interest features. Services are offered at no cost to the practitioner.

Contact Point is a national not-for-profit organization directed by a multi sectoral Board of Directors comprised of volunteers from the private, not-for-profit and educational sectors

In pockets of intense activity peppered throughout the country, after nearly a century of development and growth, much of it occurring in the last two decades, the career counselling profession is still working to define its terms. Although different words are often used in different sectors, ever so slowly a common vocabulary is emerging. A common body of knowledge has begun to come together.

From within the various sectors of the field have come program, curricula and content developers. Some practitioners continue to work within institutions. Others have moved out of education or government to work in the voluntary or not-for-profit sector, some in the private sector. In addition to program development, a few have taken on some of the administrative tasks required by the field as a whole. The profession's sense of identity and professionalism was sufficient to give rise to the development of Contact Point, an on-line resource centre for career practitioners, drawn from the community itself and tailor-made to a Canadian audience of professionals. Also, a post-secondary consortium including Wilfred Laurier University, the universities of Waterloo and Guelph, and Conestoga College would offer on-line career practitioner curricula. By the close of the century, many students were enrolled in programs across the country leading to their obtaining the qualifications of a career counsellor.

Precisely how to refer to the emerging field remains a controversial issue. To some, at least, the term "counselling" seems too limited, too therapeutic in its connotation. "The term career development is more encompassing," says Jan Basso, of the University of Waterloo. "Career development includes the whole process of helping clients with that career decision-making, in terms of doing a self-assessment, identifying the kinds of things that might be appropriate and satisfying for them in terms of working."

Laurie Edwards, from Nova Scotia's Department of Education, concurs. "A counselling model is one that would suggest a therapeutic model," she feels, "a diagnosis. It suggests there's something wrong and now we have to do an intervention. For me, career development means working together with clients on something that's important to them. Not to do problem-solving, but to figure out what a preferred future would be."

Career development as an instrument of public policy

Canada is known internationally for its high calibre of innovation in career and employment products and programs. Experts from government and education are in demand around the world and often work as consultants to countries as far afield as Oman, Romania and Chile, providing outside expertise to practitioners learning to manage their own national workforces.

UBC's Norm Amundson is one of the growing number of specialists who often work outside the country. "You realize when you step outside of Canada," Amundson says, "even to the United States, that much of the work we're doing is leading, cutting edge."

As professionals in the field have developed ways and means of measuring the effectiveness of the counselling process, the role of the profession has been raised in the hierarchy of labour market strategies.

"In the 1980s, counselling was seen by many people at the top of organizations as being something to improve the fairness of society, something to deal with disadvantaged workers, with those discriminated against in some way," says Hunter. "It was very difficult to sell it as something that would promote the efficiency of the labour market that would mean that people found jobs better and faster, and that jobs got filled better and faster than they otherwise would."

In the mid-1990s, however, the Organization of Economic Cooperation and Development (OECD) put forward the view that specific labour market policies such as job search assistance, job clubs and counselling were effective in reducing long term unemployment.

"The trend moved away from training and job creation," says Hunter. "There's a recognition that counselling can increase the efficiency of the labour market at the same time as it is increasing the fairness of the labour market."

Accurately documenting outcomes can help improve the field's standing, says the University of Lethbridge's Kris Magnussen. "Counsellors have not taken enough responsibility for documenting their impact," according to Magnussen. "They don't know how to do that very well...It's a political process but it's also a professional obligation. We have to become much better at documenting how we do a job, how effective we are. We have to be able to say, as a result of the work that I did, there were another fifty students who stayed in school."

Growth and development in Canada's career counselling community has occurred along three main streams of activity: service delivery, information and product development, and the training of professionals.

Service delivery

As the 21st century gets underway, a range of employment and career services is available across the country, many in the public sector, in government and community career and employment counselling centres, in schools, colleges and universities. Some services are available in the private sector, as well. And it is here, suggests Edmonton's

David Redekopp that the greatest potential for future growth can be found. "It's almost entirely untapped," he says. "At a rough guess, 90, maybe 95 percent of career counsellors work with the 6 percent of workers who are unemployed. Maybe 5 percent of counsellors actually work with the employed. I want to see that ratio change almost entirely. The opportunities are endless on that front."

Career information, products and tools

Canada's library of career-related information is extensive and much of it is available on-line including occupational databases, career assessment products, labour market information and sectoral studies. For example, the Myers-Briggs Type Indicator® (MBTI) is widely used by career counsellors to help clients identify their personality and temperament. Several of the country's innovative career products—such as Career Explorer and The Real Game, a curriculum based on a board game for career exploration, originally developed by Newfoundlander, Bill Barry, for his daughter's grade school class—have built strong reputations around the world.

Having sophisticated products such as these at our disposal is "something of a mixed blessing," observes Bryan Hiebert of the University of Alberta. "When you have good quality products," he notes, "if people aren't careful, they can be seduced by the product and they end up thinking that their job as career facilitator is really just to take the products and let them do the work."

Information can be distracting, as well, says Redekopp. "Sometimes it sets up an illusion of having something that actually isn't really there. It's great for statisticians and labour market analysts, and people who want to keep track of the economy as a whole…that type of information has no life, no context, no meaning and at best serves a sort of introduction to what's going on in the world of work.

"If you look at a hierarchy of data, information, knowledge and wisdom, information has its place. So does data. But information and data aren't knowledge or wisdom. There's a million ways to get knowledge and wisdom and counselling is one of them."

Early tools which became available in the 1970s to prioritize skills, knowledge and values—such as the card sorting system entitled Career Values, developed by Dick Knowdell based on Howard Figler's work—have now been replaced by more elaborate methods of data collection and analysis.

Canadian consultant and career self-management advocate Barbara Moses has created a number of tools including a Career Planning Workbook, which is now used widely in corporate culture around the world. Her books include *Career Intelligence: Mastering the New Work and Personal Realities, Career Intelligence: The 12 New Rules for Work* and *Life Success*. Additional resource materials have been developed by Youth Employment Service's Director Nancy Schaeffer including Good Job: A Young Person's guide to Finding, Landing and Loving a Job.

> The 20th century provided career counselling with many challenges and opportunities upon which to hone its craft.

Training and professional development

In the academic community, not surprisingly, expectations of levels of education are generally clearly defined. At times, these are established by provincial guidelines; at other times, they are set by the institution or school board. Within the educational system, a master's degree is generally needed to work as a career counsellor or a career educator.

For many within the career counselling and career development community embracing similar expectations would have significant implications. The belt tightening of public sector funders during the latter part of the century had pushed the concept of fiscal accountability onto the front burner of all service providers (not-for-profit and profit) seeking to provide federally funded fee-for-service programs. Programs were evaluated more rigorously, with particular emphasis on tangible, measurable outcomes, in terms of client placement and program delivery standards. This climate served to raise once again within the career practitioner community the issue of credentials as a way of increasing the credibility of the profession (and to strengthen a proponent's case for a fee for service relationship or the potential receipt of public funds). Should such credentials be established as a standard in other sectors? Some feel strongly that they should. Others disagree. One of the dilemmas the profession faced in addressing this question was what some saw as its greatest strength: the diversity of backgrounds and special interests and expertise of the career practitioner. In fact, there was no one single environment in which a member of the profession could be found, nor one direct educational path that took them there. This variety of settings (government, community agency, educational institution, private sector) and backgrounds of the counsellors themselves (from members of the clergy to psychologists) made accreditation a challenge. In addition, some counsellors and practitioners are not convinced that their personal credentials determine and/or impact client outcomes.

Despite the dedicated efforts of people like Frank Lawson to encourage the availability of professional development, however, there remains a dearth of graduate or post-graduate studies. The most active training programs for those in the field are found in community colleges, either as full-time diploma or certificate programs, or part-time courses through continuing education and distance learning. Opportunities for graduates are expanding, says Bill O'Byrne, of Sir Sanford Fleming College in Peterborough, which offered one of the first employment and career counselling programs in the country. Students in the class of 2000 have all found work in the field, he reports with considerable satisfaction.

Many career counsellors who identify themselves as professionals are, in fact, without graduate training and do outstanding work, says outplacement pioneer, Murray Axmith. "The common ground is who the counsellor is as a person...A person who has a lot of sensitivity, who reads people well, who is genuine, who has a quest to know and understand, who has empathy and who is nonjudgmental—these are the counselling skills that underpin everything."

A Canadian chapter of the International Association of Career Management Professionals was established early in the 1990s. "One of the things that has developed is a move toward certification of professionals in the corporate area," Axmith points out. "And that involved taking in special programs and conferences, writing papers and building experience. In order to get certified, people had to have specific experience, but they also had to contribute to the field."

Emphasis on academic credentials is a concern of both profit and not-for-profit counsellors and practitioners who continue to focus on client outcomes and program delivery, rather than on the credentials of individual counsellors or practitioners. The CFC's Elizabeth McTavish put forward a view in the 1980s that reflects Murray Axmith's view today: "Varied and rich life experience, intelligence and the ability to learn from that experience, coupled with rapport with the client are surely the essence of counselling," she said.

Implications of technology in career development as a profession

Technological advancements have had an enormous impact on the practice of career counselling. The availability of the Internet and e-mail make job searching much more comprehensive for job seekers and facilitate the easy review of applicants by potential employers. On-line job banks, specialized web sites and the plethora of information available can be overwhelming. The presence of the technology has also required career counsellors to be specially trained, so that they, in turn, can assist their clients in accessing what the Internet has to offer.

Telecommunication technology has also enhanced career counselling services. Where distance separates clients from counsellors, teleconferencing can be used to great advantage. For some provinces, for instance Newfoundland where the provision of services is made almost impossible to outlying areas, teleconferencing has been able to bring services to Canadians across the province. This, together with the Internet, has permitted the development of telecareer development, bringing a challenge of its own, as counsellors themselves must adapt to the effects of the new global economy and to the impact of technology in the workplace.

Keltie Creed, one of the first full-time e-counsellors says, "Ironically, although counselling is a profession that teaches people how to understand and cope with transition and change, a significant number of us have been resistant to introducing technology into our practice. Perhaps this is the ordeal, the test that will temper us and bring the field from an unformed childhood to maturity."

In 1997, Canada was the first country to fund employment and career counselling via the Internet. The Canadian Council on Rehabilitation and Work offered free e-counselling using chat technology for anyone who did not have access to a counsellor in person. Although initially conceived as a service for individuals with disabilities who were isolated, it quickly became evident that the general public also wanted this option. People who live in the north or other rural areas preferred being able to talk directly to a counsellor without travelling; homemakers with children did not have to arrange childcare; some youth were more comfortable expressing themselves through keyboards; and there was a great demand for assistance from people hoping to immigrate or return to Canada.

There were also requests from the U.S. and Europe to train counsellors in how to adapt their counselling techniques to the medium.

However, most counsellors were apprehensive about the concept. Although many worked from cubicles rather than private offices or in group settings, they worried about hackers and confidentiality. The majority wondered about lack of non-verbal cues, feeling that they could not communicate solely through text. Still others were intimidated by technology and stated simply that the day they had to use a computer would be the day they would seek a career counsellor themselves.

Yet within a few short years, most counsellors routinely refer clients to use on-line job banks and to research companies using the Internet; they are gaining comfort using it themselves. With more than a million resumes being added to databanks on the Internet each month, counsellors need to be able to advise job seekers on the pros and cons of various formats for electronic resumes and portfolios. This includes attachments, submissions through company web sites, and helping clients critique their home pages or CD ROM portfolios. Requests for help with hypertext resumes (live links on web sites or disc) have increased on a daily basis since 1998. We are growing past the era of resumes and entering into the age of personal marketing.

"Counsellors will also be working with more clients who are very comfortable with web-based communication such as instant messaging and text messaging via cell phone or pagers. They may be using these mediums for e-mentoring, networking or information interviews. In some professions, they are already doing their proficiency tests online and having pre-screening or initial interviews via chat, web-cam or telephony (telephone via Internet). This is partially to test technical skills of the applicant but has also become part of some corporate cultures. Counsellors and coaches need to be prepared to increase computer literacy and our skill sets to keep pace with the corporate world," says Keltie Creed.

Marc Verhoeve, cybertraining consultant, agrees. He predicts a need for "more techno-literate counsellors to service clients who are already there; increased demand for us to increase our literacy in standardized testing, either 'bark-based' or web-based (e.g., JVIS.com); increased emphasis on EAPs (Employee Assistance Programs) to service employees/associates in large firms, ideally web-based to provide the service to all international branches; and more e-conferenced professional development to allow helping professionals to tap the expertise of consultants without having to invest the time and money to travel to grow professionally."

Both Creed and Verhoeve recognize the need to update our ethics guidelines and to educate both the counselling field and the public about safeguards and precautions when working on-line. However, similar concerns were voiced when professionals first began communicating with

> "Let's forget about the legal implications for a moment and focus on the quality of counselling through electronic means. How effective can your relationship be with your client if you never see their face? (This presumes you do not have video conferencing…) Think about all the nuances of facial expression and body reactions that you may never catch. Considering the power of non-verbal cues, this would be a real detriment to interpretation and bonding."
>
> Mark Swartz MBA, Author and Consultant, "Cyber Counselling: Panacea or can of worms?" in *Technology and Career and Employment Counselling: A Compendium of Thought*, published by The Counselling Foundation of Canada, January 1998.

clients via the telephone and it soon became evident that the benefits far exceeded the risks.

They also predict that counsellors will need to prepare themselves for a more global clientele, so cultural sensitivity and diversity training will need to be included in our own continual learning. Probably there will also be a demand for more emphasis on holistic career/lifestyle counselling and stress management, especially factoring in the eldercare mandate.

Technology is having a profound impact on the working life of Canadians, which in turn causes the counselling paradigm to shift. There will always be a demand for individual assistance, but it may not always be restricted by location. High speed Internet access has already made teleconferencing and web broadcasting much easier and more affordable. Software advancements make building and editing web-based portfolios and resumes as easy as word processing. Data retrieval services and search software offer information on careers and industries that was previously inaccessible. Disability, age and geographic location become unique qualities rather than barriers. Time becomes more elastic, as both synchronous and asynchronous communication options are available. Resources appear to be unlimited. Technology may been seen as an ordeal, a functional tool or an exciting adventure. However, it has also been a catalyst moving the counselling profession through the coming of age into maturity.

The role of government

Although government funding has done much to help build the field, a number of knots in the public purse strings have tended to thwart it as well. Funding patterns changed dramatically during the 1990s. Despite a growing understanding of the demands of a knowledge society and a learning culture, educational budgets were cut, along with career and employment programs, materials and staff.

Community-based programs tend to be insecure. Government funds come packaged in yearly contracts. At the same time, funding policies are subject to change—changes in human resource management strategies, changes in political regimes and philosophies and changes as internal problems restructure government bureaucracies. Nor are government programs always flexible enough to deal with some of the deep problems of the people on the outer fringes of Canadian society.

"In our drive—some would say obsession—for accountability, we've designed programs that don't work for marginalized people with multiple barriers," says Martin Garber-Conrad of the Edmonton City Centre Church Corporation.

Garber-Conrad is the motivating force behind Edmonton's landmark program for severely-at-risk youth, Kids In the Hall. Many of the people he works to help do not fit well into traditional employment or social programs, he says, because their needs are "complex, deep and long-standing. It's not wrong to expect measurable outcomes. But we define them in the broad mainstream kind of categories and it's very difficult to 'succeed' with people with multiple barriers to employment."

Success for government-sponsored employment programs generally has been defined in fairly simplistic terms, a tally of the number of "placements," without an attempt to assess the quality and longevity of those placements. Faced with the need to "place" people in order to continue receiving funding, program developers tend to stay away from marginalized people like street kids, says Garber-Conrad. "The higher the risk, the more problems they're likely to have, the greater the difficulty there is in succeeding."

Decisions made at national headquarters or regional headquarters tend to be "one size fits all," according to employment service historian John Hunter. "The decision-making is getting pushed down," says Hunter, who views the devolution of labour force training and development to the provinces and communities as a positive move.

"What you really want to have is a bundle of measures that you can employ and pick and choose among, depending on the need," he says. "Flexibility will be the ultimate result. If you have a layoff in a mine where the ore has been depleted, you need different kinds of measures than you do if a company is temporarily shut down because of excess inventory. Training and other services are being devolved to the levels of the country where reasonable decisions can be made by people who know the best mix of labour market measures to deal with labour market problems." However, the jury is still out on the impact of the withdrawal of the federal government from providing the extent of national leadership they had in the past in this field.

An evolving national community

In this period of transition, as the federal government continues to offload many of its training, employment and career services to the provinces, the career counselling community must struggle to adapt. Some career practitioners complain that devolution has left the field fractured and suffering from a loss of national leadership. And yet, as funding cuts have made direct services harder and harder to provide, technology has in many ways enhanced the abilities of the profession to provide reliable career selection information by way of the Internet.

Some applaud the creative initiatives underway to advance the field, perhaps in spite or because of the withdrawal of the federal government. Conflicting realities such as these are part of "an era of paradox," in Norm Amundson's view. "No longer are we saying either-or; we're saying both. There is this interaction going on and it can't be either one or the other, but it needs to be some creative integration that pulls both sides together."

In the career counselling community, creative integration to pull the field together can be found in national forums. NATCON has become increasingly important as an annual meeting place for practitioners, theorists and program developers from across the country. The Canadian Career Information Partnership, established in 1992, now meets several times a year, bringing together representatives from the provinces, territories and the federal government to work on product development and national initiatives.

Many challenges ahead

Accountability. Outcomes. Professional standards. Devolution. Funding restrictions. Skill development. International collaboration. New technologies. These are some, at least, of the issues a new generation of Canadian career practitioners will have face in the years ahead.

To meet challenges of this kind, new understanding will be needed and new learning. The field will have to accept the risks and opportunities inherent in this critical moment of growth and development and find ways to coalesce around collective directions, in order to move ahead as a profession.

To the many people in the field who have seen this and recognized the significance of the moment at which the field now stands, this means a new awareness, an evolution in understanding as individual practitioners and as a community. Devolution, the need to deal with one's own thinking about skills, the role of funding, the value of contributions from each of the sectors within which counselling occurs, communication, and the quality of the thoughts that are exchanged—all of these factors will determine the degree to which the profession will be able to work together and develop the field.

Perhaps the greatest opportunity for the profession is the introduction of technologies that may make cyber-counselling more commonplace. As a means of finding labour market information, referring clients and matching skills with requirements, the electronic highway presents career counselling with a whole new realm of possibilities. Perhaps one of the principal benefits the Internet brings—as seen through the success of Contact Point—is the value of creating a virtual meeting place, where career practitioners from every setting and background can share insight and experience with the larger career development community.

The future

We leave the final word to some of the people in the field:

"There's excitement in this field," says Barry Day. "When you're in a relatively new discipline, there's an excitement about innovation. And everybody gets involved."

"Together," as Laurie Edwards puts it, "we can do much more work than we can as little islands."

"Certainly we have developed, in many ways, a much more sophisticated perspective," according to Vance Peavy, "and certainly things are better in some ways than they were but I don't like the concept of maturation too much. I don't think career counselling or any counselling ever will be mature. I hope not. What I hope is that there is a continuing, evolving reflection on itself, making itself better, changing as society changes, as the lives of people change. When the lives of people change, then things like counselling must also change, in order to be appropriate and sensible in the new context."

"There's been this increase in the esteem of the field," says Bryan Hiebert, "but also in the pride that people feel working in the area. I think it's because now we've got a critical brain pool. And so we've got a certain amount of synergy happening. And when creative people get together, magic happens."

"Increasingly, more and more practitioners are utilizing online learning and networking tools to assist them in the work they do," states Rizwan Ibrahim, Executive Director, Contact Point. "Finding a balance between their hectic workloads and beneficial easy-to-access online tools will be their challenge in the years to come."

Mark Swartz, Career Consultant, speaker and author concurs: "The possibilities are, in fact, very exciting – for those who embrace the technologies and use them appropriately."

"Career counselling is a journey," comments Wendy Woods, in her capacity as President of the Ontario Association of Youth Employment Centres. "Over the next few years, it will be imperative that counsellors servicing young people be knowledgeable of the difficulties encountered in a changing economy and work environment, responsive to client needs and creative in applying counselling processes." Further, Woods urges that, "as we continue the journey, we need to revel in the diversity of the young people we meet, as well as the diversity of the processes that we apply, so that we are equipped to assist clients in reaching their goals."

"We are on the cutting edge of recognizing that what we do is critical to the future of Canadian society," says Robert Shea, founding editor of the Canadian Journal of Career Development. "I believe the future of career development is creating and disseminating new knowledge about careers research in Canada. We must partner with all sectors involved in the Canadian career community. We're on the cusp of something great."

"Our future at The Counselling Foundation of Canada will include continuing to look at the barriers that keep individual Canadians from attaining their full potential," envisions Donald Lawson, Chairman of the Foundation. "We will continue to seek out new and creative approaches to providing career counselling and make the necessary investments to make things happen."

The 20th century provided career counselling with a myriad of challenges and opportunities upon which to hone its craft. The future will no doubt bring a new set of challenges and opportunities, upon which the profession is equipped to capitalize.

The Counselling Foundation of Canada

The Counselling Foundation of Canada (CFC), a family foundation funded by Frank G. Lawson and his estate, dates back to the early 1940s. The stimulus for its establishment was rooted in two issues: too many young people were being inappropriately lodged in mental institutions; and men released from the armed services required assistance in seeking a new vocation.

Formally incorporated in 1959, Frank Lawson's purpose in establishing the Foundation was to create and enrich counselling programs and improve the technical skills of counsellors. As founder and chair from 1959-1984, Frank Lawson, a stock broker, took an active and personal role in searching out and developing granting opportunities which would enhance the self-perception of young people in such a way that they would not hesitate to commit themselves to the dignity of work with the expectation that they would be successful. Every grant request was reviewed as rigorously as any stock purchase. Every grant approved was an investment towards ensuring the provision of counselling services to young people in Canada.

At the time of Frank Lawson's death in 1984, all post-secondary educational institutions had a counselling service. A number of career development theories had been developed. High school guidance systems were in place and some students even reported that some of them were helpful.

Frank's son, Donald G. Lawson, assumed responsibility as the Chair of the Foundation in 1984 when he established a seven member Board of Directors, four of whom are family members, to govern the CFC as it worked towards its goal of encouraging the development of positive growth in the lives of individuals and the health of our communities.

During its forty-year history, The Counselling Foundation of Canada has provided over $31 million dollars in community investment grants to registered charitable organizations. Grants have been provided to community not-for-profit agencies, universities, colleges, primary and secondary schools, and other focus educational organizations. Approximately 89 percent of this community investment has been made since 1985.

Like many agencies, organizations and communities, the Board and Members of the Foundation have recognized the importance of a growing number of emerging social issues, which have tremendous significance for the development of human resources in Canada. While the traditional focus of counselling and career development remains ever present, the Foundation has expanded its focus to include factors that affect future employability. This has brought a broad range of issues, encompassing all ages from children at risk to adults wishing to enter or re-enter the workforce, into the realm of community investments made by The Counselling Foundation of Canada.

Today, as in the past, active interventions are the preferred investment. There is a purpose to be achieved with each grant and that purpose is directly related to an increase in the economic and social wealth and productivity of the individual and the community.

In the late 1950s, it became evident that the growing demand for counselling psychologists could not be met unless Canadian universities were persuaded to alter their programs in teaching psychology to place more emphasis on applied studies. Grants were made to this end. Grants to universities also focused on improving the quality of career information and counselling resources available to students. In total, twenty-one Canadian universities received multi-year funding to establish and/or enhance what has evolved into the on-campus Student Placement and Career Centre and/or Psychological Services. The university sector remained a primary recipient of grants until the early 1990s.

It was recognized that parish ministers were frequently the only persons providing any form of counselling in their communities. It was believed enhancement in the training of ministers in family and marriage counselling would be beneficial. Grants included the provision of counselling services and curriculum development at the applicable institutions.

The mid-1980s saw a strategic increase in the investments made in community-based, not-for-profit agencies and organizations. Community agencies were perceived to be on the front line of the employment issues. Having acknowledged the difficulties experienced by many maturing in economic hardship, The Counselling Foundation of Canada focussed more sharply on those issues which would contribute to total development of young people. Issues dealing with youths at risk, particularly of dropping out of school, were met with approaches of in-school behavioural counselling, anti-racism programs, the recruitment of volunteer mentors to interact with youths as well as programs to encourage young people to function as volunteers in their community.

In 1995, based on the success of a limited number of pilot projects and with the encouragement of its members, The Counselling Foundation of Canada revised its statement of purpose to focus some resources on parenting and early childhood development. Since then, significant resources have been invested in the community-based, not-for-profit sector for programs and services to children and families most at risk.

The goals of the Foundation:

- To promote effective delivery of counselling through reputable and credible existing institutions (education, religious and community) to individuals involved in the process of career development;
- To encourage and support information and evaluation centres for career counselling;
- To work towards the professionalization of counselling and promote public education which clarifies the role and qualifications of counsellors; and
- To encourage and support programs which contribute to healthy child development especially for those groups of parents and children known to be at greatest risk.

Projects which partner community resources are preferred. All grants are time limited subject to annual review. The order of priority for grants, according to geographic location, is Toronto, Ontario and Canada. Grants are not made for research projects, building funds, emergency funds, deficit financing, endowment funds, equipment funds, mass fundraising appeals, long-term funding, capital funds, awards, fellowships, bursaries, or to individuals.

Bibliography

Mahjetahwin Meekunaung Beginning on the Path Career Learning Program (Anishinabek Educational Institute).

Technology and Career and Employment Counselling: A Compendium of Thoughts (Toronto: The Counselling Foundation of Canada).

Nancy Adamson, *Career Counselling in Canada Sectoral Outline: Corporate* (Toronto: The Counselling Foundation of Canada).

Craig Brown, *ed., The Illustrated History of Canada* (Toronto: Key Porter).

Irene Canivet, *Career Counselling in Canada Sectoral Outline: Education* (Toronto: The Counselling Foundation of Canada).

Daniel Denis, *Career Counselling in Canada Sectoral Outline: Not-for-profit Organizations* (Toronto: The Counselling Foundation of Canada).

Alvin Finkel and Margaret Conrad, *History of the Canadian Peoples 1867 to the Present* (Toronto: Copp Clark Ltd.).

John Hunter, *The Employment Challenge: Federal employment policies and programs 1900-1990* (Ottawa: Government of Canada).

Mark Kingwell and Christopher Moore, *Canada Our Century* (Toronto: Doubleday Canada).

Laurel Sefton Macdowell and Ian Radforth, eds., *Canadian Working Class History: Selected Readings 2nd edition* (Toronto: Canadian Scholars' Press, Inc.).

Harvey Mandel, *Peers as Mentors* (Toronto: The Counselling Foundation of Canada).

Aaron Miester, *Career Counselling in Canada Sectoral Outline: Labour* (Toronto: The Counselling Foundation of Canada).

Desmond Morton, *A Short History of Canada 3rd edition* (Toronto: McClelland & Stewart).

Nancy Schaefer, *Good Job!* (Toronto: Stoddart)

Frank Schmidt and Grace Gerrard, ed, *Opening Doors: Blind and Visually Impaired People and Work.* (Toronto: Canadian National Institute for the Blind, 1989)

Joanne Sobkow, *Career Counselling in Canada Sectoral Outline: Government* (Toronto: The Counselling Foundation of Canada).

Super, D. E. *"A Life-Span, Life-Space Approach to Career Development"* in D. Brown & Brooks, L., *Career Choice and Development 2nd ed.* (San Francisco: Jossey-Bass, 2000).

Pauline Wong, *The History of Career Counselling* (Youth Education Sector).

Darius R. Young, *An Historical Survey of Vocational Education in Canada* (North York: Captus Press)